Joseph Skipsey

Carols from the Coal Fields

And other Songs and Ballads

Joseph Skipsey

Carols from the Coal Fields
And other Songs and Ballads

ISBN/EAN: 9783744775557

Printed in Europe, USA, Canada, Australia, Japan

Cover: Foto ©Thomas Meinert / pixelio.de

More available books at **www.hansebooks.com**

CAROLS

FROM

THE COAL-FIELDS:

AND OTHER

SONGS AND BALLADS.

BY

JOSEPH SKIPSEY.

All Rights Reserved.

LONDON:
WALTER SCOTT, 24 WARWICK LANE.
PATERNOSTER ROW.
1886.

INSCRIBED

TO

ROBERT SPENCE WATSON, Esq., LL.D.,

OF NEWCASTLE-UPON-TYNE,

AS A TOKEN OF

SINCERE REGARD AND AFFECTION,

BY THE AUTHOR.

Aug. 1886.

ERRATA.

Page 48, line 4, for *And*, read *That*.
Page 97, line 12, for *may yet control*, read *can not control*.
Page 169, line 11, for *no*, read *nor*.
Page 197, line 3, for *blood-rose*, read *blood-dyed rose*.

CONTENTS.

	PAGE
Lo, A Fairy	1
My Merry Bird	2
Mother Wept	3
Thistle and Nettle	4
Mary of Crofton	16
The Star and The Meteor	17
Willy and Jinny	17
Hey Robin	18
Polly and Harry	19
Young Fanny	20
The Hartley Calamity	21
The Proud One's Doom	25
Annie Lee	26
Bereaved	27
The Wilted Leaf	36
Dora Dee	37

CONTENTS.

	PAGE
The Lad of Bebside	38
Meg Goldlocks	39
Poor Rose	40
Rosa Rea	43
Undeceived	45
The Three Maidens	46
The Breezelet	47
The Fatal Errand	48
The Ring	49
Stanzas	56
Lo, the Day	57
The Hell Broth	58
The Reign of Gold	61
Daffodil and Daisy	63
A Lullaby	64
The Collier Lad	65
The Seaton Terrace Lass	68
Wonder-Bound	70
Kit Clark	71
My Loved One	72
The Seer	73
Tit-for-Tat	77
Annie	78
Away to the Well	79
Sympathy	80
Nanny to Bessy	81

CONTENTS.

	PAGE
Love without Hope	83
The Stars are Twinkling	90
The Question	91
The Dance	94
The Spell	95
The Angel Mother	96
Robin Redbreast	100
Arachne	101
The Theft	106
Lost at the Fair	107
"Get Up"	108
The Bridal Gift	109
The Mystic Lyre	111
The Dewdrop	113
Away to the Fair	114
Music	117
The Butterfly	119
Slighted	120
The Modest Maid	122
The Outcast Flower	123
The Moth	125
The Toast	126
Two Hazel Eyes	127
Omega	128
The Oracle	131
All is Vanity	132

CONTENTS.

	PAGE
The Parties	134
The Social Glass	135
A Word of Good Cheer	136
My Little Boy	139
The Stained Lily	140
The Violet and the Rose	141
The Resolve	142
God and the Right	143
The Brooklet	145
Uncle Bob	146
Bubble-Blowing	154
The Vision	156
I'm A-weary	158
The Two Visions	158
The Songstress	159
She is not Fashioned	160
The Crushed Aspirer	161
The Mysterious Rider	162
An Error	162
Becky Sharp—	
I. The Ditty	163
II. Consolation	163
III. The Precious Pearl	164
IV. The Toast	164
Misfortune	165
Io Pæan	167

CONTENTS.

	PAGE
Little Anna	169
Cruel Anna	171
Baloo	173
The Ruin	174
Life and Death	175
The Summer Breezelet	176
Alas!	177
Lotty Hay	178
Dolly Dare	180
Lilly and Willy	182
Barbara Bell	184
The Death of Cleopatra	186
The Charmer	190
The Broken Spell	191
The Fairies' Adieu	192

THE MAGIC GLASS.

I. The Inner Harp	193
II. The Fair Rower	193
III. The Lucky Hour	194
IV. The Assurance	194
V. The Secret	195
VI. The Bugle-Horn	195
VII. The Pearl	196

CONTENTS.

	PAGE
VIII. The Two-fold Surprise	196
IX. The Return	197
X. The Bee and the Rose	197
XI. The Rose's Complaint	198
XII. The Echo	198
XIII. The Minstrel	199
XIV. The Seen and the Unseen	199
XV. The Fair Thief	200
XVI. The Two Mirrors	200
XVII. The One Solace	201
XVIII. The Syren	201
XIX. The Cloud	202
XX. The Songstress	202

THE GOLDEN BOWL.

I. The Bowl	203
II. The Right Thing	203
III. The Tower	204
IV. Too True	204
V. Not Jealous	205
VI. Jack the Rover	205
VII. Extreme Kindness	206
VIII. Steeds and their Riders	206
IX. Uncouth Things	207
X. What Else?	207

CONTENTS.

	PAGE
XI. Hag Night	208
XII. Just the Way	208
XIII. The Witch-Glass	209
XIV. Not the Bird	209
XV. Dame Malice	210
XVI. Rumour	210
XVII. The Critics	211
XVIII. The Petition	211
XIX. Billy Taylor	212
XX. Just So	212

THE POSY-GIFT.

I. You quite mistake the sprite you chase	213
II. He giggled at the thought, and had	213
III. Another stave I'll never rave	214
IV. Ha, ha! last night I served you right	214
V. These jewels left her very hand	215
VI Come, pretty flowers, and drink my tears	215
VII. What fancies throng into the mind	216
VIII. One fancy kicks another's heel	216
IX. Once more, sweet Muse, a fancy choose	217
X. Go, Musie, go! you like, I know	217
XI. These flowers that so reflect the grace	218
XII. All things of beauty seek to draw	218

	PAGE
XIII. Come, let me smell thee, lily-bell	219
XIV. These lovely blooms, their rich perfumes	219
XV. Blind as the wretch who mock'd my flowers	220
XVI. O, dear, dear, dear! what shall I do?	220
XVII. Ha, ha! at last you're fetter'd fast	221
XVIII. With Common Sense one might dispense	221
XIX. 'Tis quite a treat, as singer knows	222
XX. My Song must end; and now I'll send	222
A Cry for Poland	223
A Golden Lot	224
To a Startled Bird	224

PSYCHIC POEMS.

I. The Vital Spark	325
II. The Downfall of Mammon	228
III. The Riddle Read	232
IV. The Mission	235
V. Behind the Veil	240
VI. What is Man?	244
VII. The Soul's Hereafter	247
VIII. The Inner Conflict	248
IX. The Thought Toiler	252
X. The Guardian Angel	254
Note	255, 256

THE SINGER.

What tho', in bleak Northumbria's mines,
    His better part of life hath flown,
A planet's shone on him, and shines,
    To Fortune's darlings seldom known;

And while his outer lot is grim,
    His soul, with light and rapture fraught,
Oft will a carol trill, or hymn
    In deeper tones the deeper thought.

Carols, Songs, and Ballads.

LO, A FAIRY.

Lo, a fairy on a day
Came and bore my heart away;
But as she secured her prize,
Sweetest smiles illumed her eyes.
　And, hey, lerry O !

From that moment my career
Lay thro' dells and dingles, where
Pleasure blossom'd out of pain—
Where Joy sang her golden strain,
　Hey, hey, lerry O !

MY MERRY BIRD.

I HAD a merry bird
   Who sung a merry song,
And take it on my word,
   The day it was not long
In presence of my bird with its merry, merry song.

   Did fortune strew my way
      With crosses, which, to bear,
   Had rendered me a prey
      To sorrow or despair—
My birdie trilled its lay, and they vanished into air.

   And thus went things with me,
      Till lo, with sudden sweep,
   Death came across the lea
      And laid my bird asleep;
And ever since that hour I've done nought but sigh
   and weep.

⚹ MOTHER WEPT.

Mother wept, and father sighed ;
    With delight a-glow
Cried the lad, " To-morrow," cried.
    " To the pit I go."

Up and down the place he sped,—
    Greeted old and young,
Far and wide the tidings spread,—
    Clapt his hands and sung.

Came his cronies some to gaze
    Wrapt in wonder ; some
Free with counsel ; some with praise ;
    Some with envy dumb.

" May he," many a gossip cried,
    " Be from peril kept ; "
Father hid his face and sighed,
    Mother turned and wept.

THISTLE AND NETTLE.

'TWAS on a night, with sleet and snow
   From out the north a tempest blew
When Thistle gathered nerve to go
   The little Nettle's self to woo.

Within her father's cottage soon
   He found the ever-dreaded maid;
She then was knitting to a tune
   The wind upon the window played

His errand known, she, with a frown,
   Up from the oaken table sprung,
Down took the broom and swept the room,
   While like a bell her clapper rung.

" Have I not seen enough to be
   Convinced for ever, soon or late,
The maid shall rue the moment she
   Attendeth to a wooer's prate ?

"How long ago since Phemie Hay
   To Harry at the Mill fell wrong ?
How long since Hall a prank did play
   On silly Nelly Brown ?—how long ?

"How long ago since Adam Smith
  Wooed Annie on the Moor, and left
The lassie with a stain? yea, with
  A heart of every hope bereft?

"But what need instance cases? lo!
  Have I not heard thee chaunt the lay,
'The fraud of men was ever so
  Since summer first was leafy?' eh?

"When men are to be trusted, then,
  —But never may that time befall;
Of five times five-and-twenty men,
  There's barely five are men at all.

"Before the timid maid they'll fall,
  And smile and weep and sigh and sue,
Till once they get her in their thrall,
  And then she's doomed her lot to rue.

"For her a subtle snare they weave,
  And when the bonny bird is caught,
Then, then they giggle in their sleeve;
  Then laugh to scorn the ill they've wrought.

"As other weary winds, they woo
  The bloom its treasures to unfold;
Extract its wealth—their way pursue,
  And leave her pining on the wold.

"When poppies fell like lilies smell,
    When cherries grow on brambles, when—
When grapes adorn the common thorn,
    Then women may have faith in men.

"Then may we hear what they may swear;
    Till then, sir, know I'm on my guard,
And he, the loon that brings me down,
    He, he'll be pardoned, on my word."

Thus for an hour her tongue was heard;
    By this, her words grown faint and few,
She raised the broom at every word,
    And thumped the floor to prove it true.

In ardent words the youth replied:—
    "Dread hollow-hearted guile thou must;
But deem not all of honour void,
    Nor punish all with thy mistrust.

"A few, not all, the lash have earn'd,
    Let but that few the lash assail;
The world were topsy-turvy turned,
    Did not some sense of right prevail.

"Destroy the weed, but spare the flower;
    Consume the chaff, but keep the grain;
Nor harry one who'd die before
    He'd give thy little finger pain."

On hearing this, she sat her down,
　　Took up her needlework again,
And tho' she strove to wear a frown,
　　Made answer in a milder strain.

" Forego thy quest.　Deceitful words
　　May yet, as they have been, may be,
A fatal lure to lighter birds ;
　　They'll never prove the like to me.

" Still by my chastity I vow,
　　As I have kept the cheat at bay,
So, should I keep my senses, so
　　I'll keep him till my dying day.

" The best that man can do or say,
　　The love of gold or rubies rare,—
Not all that wealth can furnish, may
　　Once lure to leave me in a snare.

" So end thy quest."　He only prest
　　His ardent suit the more, while she
At every word he uttered, garr'd
　　Her fleeing needles faster flee.

" My quest by honour's justified ;
　　I long have eyed and found thee still
The maid I'd like to be my bride ;
　　Would I could say the maid that will.

"Hadst thou but been a daffodil
  That with the breezes sport and play,
For all thy suitor valued, still
  Thou so hadst danced thy life away.

"But thou so fair art chaste." Thus he
  Unto her answer answers e'er,
And that too in a way that she
  Must will or nill his answer hear.

And then a chair he'd ta'en, his chair
  Unto her side he nearer drew;
Recurr'd to memories sweet and rare,
  And in a softer key did woo.

"Must all the passion which I've sought
  So long to hide be paid with scorn?
A heart with pure affection fraught
  Be doomed a hopeless love to mourn?

"And must thou still its homage spurn?
  And must thou still my suit reject?
And be to me this cruel thorn?
  Reflect upon the past, reflect!

"A time there was, and time shall pass
  To me ere that forgotten be,
When side by side from tide to tide
  We played and sported on the lea.

"Ay, then have I not chased the bee
From bloom to bloom—oft chased and caught,
And having drawn its sting in glee,
To thee the little body brought?

"Then when a bloom of rarer dyes
Into my busy fingers fell,
To whom was reached the lucky prize?
Can not thy recollection tell?

"As oft away as summer went,
Who pulled with thee the haw, bright, brown—
Brown as thy own bright eyes—and bent
For thee the richest branches down?

"With blooms I've graced thy yellow hair,
With berries filled thy lap, thy hand,—
That hand as alabaster fair—
Had every gift at my command.

"Nay, tho' to others dour, yet meek
I ever was to thee, and kind,
And when we played at hide-and-seek,
I hid where thou would'st seek to find

"Upon the play-ground still unmatched
Was I, unless my loved one played;
And then it seem'd to those who watched,
My failures were on purpose made.

"As sure as e'er a race began,
    The palm was mine unless she joined,
And then I always was out-ran,
    For still with her I lagged behind.

"The ball I drove to others, mocked
    Their efforts to arrest its flight;
But when my ball to her was knocked,
    It would upon her lap alight.

"None, up and down so well I bobbed,
    To skip the rope with me would try;
Did she attempt? my skill was robbed;
    Another skipped her out—not I.

"At play thus was't; but childhood past,
    And e'er the lasses reach their teens,
Atween them and the lads a vast
    Mysterious distance intervenes.

"They seldom on the green appear
    In careless sport and play; and if
They join the throng erect they wear
    Their head, and still their air is stiff—

"They ail they know not what. And such
    The change that on my lassie fell;
Then would she shrink my hand to touch,
    And I half feared her touch as well.

"Had I changed too? This, I can tell,—
That touch o'er me a spell would cast;
And did I pass her in the dell,
With slow and snail-like pace I pass'd.

"Her voice had lost its former ring,
Yet, in that voice such power was flung,
I better liked to hear her sing,
Than when of old to me she sung.

"Her touch, her tone, would make or mar
My bliss, and tho' with all my skill
I strove to please, and please but her,
I in her presence blundered still.

"When by the hearth she sewing sat,
Did I to thread her needle try?
Still, still my heart played pit-a-pat,
And still I miss'd the needle's eye.

"As with the needle-threading, so
We with the skein a-winding fared,
And Auntie's dreaded tongue would go
Before the dancing end appeared.

"'What ails the lass?' she often said—
'She's sound asleep!' once said, and flew,
And snatched and snapt the tangled thread,
While I—I know not how—withdrew.

"Away, too, fled those hours! Alack!
　　They came and went like visions rare,
To mock the heart, delude and wrack,
　　And leave the gazer in despair.

"Ah, less—tho' sun-illumed—less fair
　　The blobs that dance adown the burn,
And let them burst they'll re-appear
　　Ere those delightsome hours return.

"Yet they may live in thought, and could
　　They live in Nettle's thought again,
Would she not change her bearing? would—
　　Would she not change this bitter strain?

"Would she her lover still disdain?
　　Would she continue thus to gall
And put him to this cruel pain?
　　—Recall to mind the past, recall!"

Thus onward, on, his ditty flows,
　　Until—her ruffled brow is sleek,—
Till, lo! the lily drives the rose,
　　The rose the lily from her cheek.

And now the iron, sparkling hot,
　　Around with might and main he swings,
And down upon the proper spot
　　With bang on bang the hammer brings

"O, be my suit but undenied,
  And, ere the moon is on the wane,
A knot shall by the priest be tied,
  The priest shall never loose again.

" In heart and hand excell'd by none,
  Henceforth I'd front the ills of life;
And every victory I won
  Should be a jewel for my wife.

"So should the people of the dell,
  When they convened to gossip, say
For harmony we bore the bell—
  And bore it with a grace away.

"Nay, lift thy head, be not ashamed,
  If thus to feel—and thus, and O :—
As matters sinful might be blamed,
  Our saints were sinners long ago."

Deep silence here ensued. The cat,
  That lately to the nook had crept
To mark the sequel of their chat,
  Came forth—lay on the hearth and slept.

The needles bright, that left and right,
  As if with elfish glee possest,
Had gleamed and glanced, and frisked and danced,
  In quiet on her apron rest.

In concert with the storm within,
  The storm without forbears to blow;
And 'tween the sailing clouds, begin
  The joyous stars to come and go.

O'er all delight and silence brood,
  While to her wooer's bosom prest,
Poor Nettle's heart beats, beats aloud
  The tune that pleases lovers best.

And Thistle's pleased and Thistle's blest,
  And Thistle's is a joy supreme;
Aye! now of Nettle's smiles possest,
  He revels in a golden dream.

Dream on, brave youth :—An hour like this
  Annuls an age of cark and strife,
And turns into a drop of bliss
  The bitter cup of human life.

The tear is by a halo gilt,
  The thorns of life are turned to flowers,
The dirge into a merry lilt,
  When love returned for love is ours.

"I've heard," in language low and soft,
  Now Nettle's heart begins to flow;—
"I've heard of honey'd tongues full oft,
  But never felt their force till now.

"Still would I fume, as day by day
   I've seen the lasses bought and sold
By some I'd scorn'd to own, had they
   Outweighed their very weight in gold.

"My hour of triumph's o'er. In vain
   Did I my fellow-maids abuse;
I've snatched the cup, and drank the bane
   Which sets me in their very shoes;

"That turns a heart of adamant
   To pliant wax; and, in my turn,
Subjects me to the bitter taunt,
   The vanquished victor's ever borne:

"That leaveth Nettle satisfied
   To leave her kith and kin, and by
Her ever-faithful Thistle's side,
   To shelter till the day they die."

MARY OF CROFTON.

Ah! a lovely jewel was Mary of Crofton,
   And now she is cold in the clay,
We think of the heart-cheering image as often
   As we pass down the old waggon way.

Her air was a magical air, and the very
   Stone heart of the stoic entranced ;
While her wee, wee feet beat a measure as merry
   As ever by damsel was danced.

Her accents enchanted ; her lay—but the silly
   Bit linnet to vie it would seek ;
And the rose in her hair was a daffadowndilly
   Compared with the rose on her cheek.

Sue, Bessy, and Kitty still ornament Crofton,
   And rich are the charms they display ;
But we miss the sweet image of Mary as often
   As we pass down the old waggon way.

THE STAR AND THE METEOR.

Directed by a little star,
　I paced towards my own loved cot,
When rushed a meteor from afar,
　And I my little guide forgot.

Bedazzled was I, and amazed,
　When out the meteor flashed, and I
Had never more my threshold paced,
　Had not that star still gleamed on high.

WILLY TO JINNY.

Duskier than the clouds that lie
'Tween the coal-pit and the sky,
Lo, how Willy whistles by
　Right cheery from the colliree.

Duskier might the laddie be
Save his coaxing coal-black e'e,
Nothing dark could Jinny see
　A-coming from the colliree.

HEY ROBIN.

(The first two lines are old.)

Hey Robin, jolly Robin,
    Tell me how thy lady doth?
Is she laughing, is she sobbing,
    Is she gay, or grave, or both?

Is she like the finch, so merry,
    Lilting in her father's hall?
Or the crow with cry a very
    Plague to each, a plague to all.

Is she like the violet breathing
    Blessings on her native place?
Or the cruel nettle scathing
    All who dare approach her grace?

Is she like the dew-drop sparkling
    When the morn peeps o'er the land?
Or the cloud in mid-air darkling,
    When a fearful storm's at hand?

Tut, to count the freaks of woman,
    Count the pebbles of the seas;
Rob, thy lady's not uncommon,
    Be or do she what she please!

POLLY AND HARRY.

Merry, lark-like, merry,
   At the break of day,
Polly meeteth Harry
   Coming down the way ;
And her lips, they quiver,
When her eyes discover
Smiles that speak—ah never
   Peace unto the May.

Merry, blythe and merry,
   'Neath the noontide ray,
Polly meeteth Harry
   Coming up the way ;
And his accents put her
Fond heart in a flutter—
And no tongue can utter
   What her looks betray.

Merry, yet so merry,
   At the close of day,
Polly spyeth Harry
   Wooing Ely Gray !
And when this she spyeth,
Lo ! her reason dieth,
And her heart rent, cryeth
   "Woe, and well-a-day !"

YOUNG FANNY.

A CHANGE hath come over young Fanny,
    The yellow-hair'd lass of the Dene—
Erewhile she look'd cosy and canny,
    But now—now, what aileth the queen ?

Erewhile she'd the bearing which blesses
    The heart of the weary and worn,
Now all Percy Main she distresses,
    And burdens the air with her scorn.

Erewhile she was sweet as the lily,
    And mild as the lamb on the lea,
Now sour as the docken, and truly
    More fierce than a tiger is she.

Erewhile she would play with the kitten,
    Averse to contention and strife,
Now Tab on the house-top is sitting
    And dare not come down for her life.

" What aileth the jewel ? " Quoth granny ;
    " What aileth the winds when they blow ?
When the reason's no secret to Fanny,
    The reason we mortals may know."

THE HARTLEY CALAMITY.

The Hartley men are noble, and
   Ye'll hear a tale of woe;
I'll tell the doom of the Hartley men—
   The year of Sixty-two.

'Twas on a Thursday morning, on
   The first month of the year,
When there befell the thing that well
   May rend the heart to hear.

Ere chanticleer with music rare
   Awakes the old homestead,
The Hartley men are up and off
   To earn their daily bread.

On, on they toil; with heat they broil,
   And streams of sweat still glue
The stour unto their skins, till they
   Are black as the coal they hew.

Now to and fro the putters go,
   The waggons to and fro,
And clang on clang of wheel and hoof
   Ring in the mine below.

The din and strife of human life
 Awake in "wall" and "board,"
When, lo! a shock is felt which makes
 Each human heart-beat heard.

Each bosom thuds, as each his duds
 Then snatches and away,
And to the distant shaft he flees
 With all the speed he may.

Each, all, they flee—by two—by three
 They seek the shaft, to seek
An answer in each other's face,
 To what they may not speak.

"Are we entombed?" they seem to ask,
 For the shaft is closed, and no
Escape have they to God's bright day
 From out the night below.

So stand in pain the Hartley men,
 And swiftly o'er them comes
The memory of home, nay, all
 That links us to our homes.

Despair at length renews their strength,
 And they the shaft must clear,
And soon the sound of mall and pick,
 Half drowns the voice of fear.

And hark! to the blow of the mall below
    Do sounds above reply ?
Hurra, hurra, for the Hartley men,
    For now their rescue's nigh.

Their rescue nigh ? The sounds of joy
    And hope have ceased, and ere
A breath is drawn a rumble's heard
    Re-drives them to despair.

Together, now behold them bow ;
    Their burden'd souls unload
In cries that never rise in vain
    Unto the living God.

Whilst yet they kneel, again they feel
    Their strength renew'd—again
The swing and the ring of the mall attest
    The might of the Hartley men.

And hark ! to the blow of the mall below
    Do sounds above reply ?
Hurra, hurra, for the Hartley men,
    For now their rescue's nigh.

But lo ! yon light, erewhile so bright,
    No longer lights the scene ;
A cloud of mist yon light hath kiss'd,
    And shorn it of its sheen.

A cloud of mist yon light hath kiss'd,
  And see! along must crawl,
Till one by one the lights are smote,
  And darkness covers all.

"O, father, till the shaft is cleared,
  Close, close beside me keep;
My eye-lids are together glued,
  And I—and I—must sleep."

"Sleep, darling, sleep, and I will keep
  Close by—heigh-ho!"—To keep
Himself awake the father strives—
  But he—he too—must sleep.

"O, brother, till the shaft is cleared,
  Close, close beside me keep;
My eye-lids are together glued,
  And I—and I—must sleep."

"Sleep, brother, sleep, and I will keep
  Close by—heigh-ho!"—To keep
Himself awake the brother strives—
  But he—he too—must sleep.

"O, mother dear! wert, wert thou near
  Whilst sleep!"—The orphan slept;
And all night long by the black pit-heap
  The mother a dumb watch kept.

And fathers, and mothers, and sisters, and brothers--
  The lover and the new-made bride—
A vigil kept for those who slept,
  From eve to morning tide.

But they slept—still sleep—in silence dread,
  Two hundred old and young,
To awake when heaven and earth have sped,
  And the last dread trumpet rung.

THE PROUD ONE'S DOOM.

" QUEEN PEARL'S own equal—nay,
  A fairer far am I," May Dewdrop said,
As Sol at break of day
  Did kiss the sparkler on her grass-blade bed.

" None may my charms resist ! "
"None," Sol still kissing answered, when alas !
The proud one turned to mist,
  And with her pride did into Lethe pass.

ANNIE LEE.

ANNIE LEE is fair and sweet—
　Fair and sweet to look upon;
But Annie's heart is all deceit,
　Therefore Annie Lee, begone.

To conceive her smiles, conceive
　Smiles the lily's self might own;
But a snare for me they'd weave:
　Therefore Annie Lee, begone.

Sweeter than a golden bell
　Sound her winning words, each one;—
From a fount of fraud they well;
　Therefore Annie Lee, begone.

In those deep blue orbs, her eyes,
　Pity's built herself a throne;
Pity! Guile in Pity's guise:
　Therefore Annie Lee, begone.

Charming Annie Lee, begone!
　Cunning Annie Lee, begone!
I'd not have thee for a world,
　Tho' so fair to look upon.

BEREAVED.

One day as I came down by Jarrow,
    Engirt by a crowd on a stone,
A woman sat moaning, and sorrow
    Seized all who took heed to her moan.

"Nay, blame not my sad lamentation,
    But oh, let," she said, " my tears flow,
Nay offer me no consolation—
    I know they are dead down below.

" I heard the dread blast and I darted
    Away on the road to the pit,
Nor stopped till my senses departed,
    And left me the wretch I here sit.

" Ah, thus let me sit," so entreated
    She those who had had her way ;
Then yet on the hard granite seated,
    Resumed her lament and did say :—

" My mother, poor body, would harry
    Me oft with a look sad and pale,
When I had determined to marry
    The dimple-chin'd lad of the dale.

"Not that she had any objection
  To one praised by each and by all;
But ay his lot caused a reflection
  That still, still her bosom would gall.

"Nay, blame not my sad lamentation;
  My mother sleeps under the yew—
She views not the dire desolation
  She dreaded one day I should view.

"Bedabbled with blood are my tresses!
  No matter! Unlock not my hand!—
When first I enjoyed his caresses,
  Their hue would his praises command.

"He'll never praise more locks nor features,
  Nor, when the long day-tide is o'er,
With me view our two happy creatures,
  With bat and with ball at the door.

"Nay, chide not. A pair either bolder
  Or better nobody could see:
They passed for a year or two older
  Than what I could prove them to be.

"Their equals for courage and action
  Were not to be found in the place;
And others might boast of attraction,
  But none had their colour or grace.

"Their feelings were such, tho' when smitten
　By scorn, oft their blood would rebel,
They wept for the little blind kitten
　Our neighbour did drown in the well.

"The same peaceful, calm, and brave bearing,
　Had still been the father's was theirs ;
And now we felt older a-wearing,
　We deemed they'd soon lighten our cares.

"So deemed I last night.　On his shoulder
　I hung and beheld them at play :
I dreamed not how soon they must moulder
　Down, down in their cold bed of clay.

"Ah, chide not.　This sad lamentation
　But endeth the burden began,
When to the whole dale's consternation,
　Our second was crushed by the van.

"That dark day the words of my mother
　In all the deep tone which had made
Me like a wind-ridden leaf dother,
　Rang like the dead bell in my head.

"Despair, the grim bird away chidden,
　Would light on the house-top again ;
But still from my husband was hidden
　Each thought that had put him to pain.

"He's pass'd from existence unharried
    By any forebodings of mine;
Nor till we the lisper had buried,
    E'er pined he. But then he did pine.

"Adown when the shadow had falling
    Across the long row gable-end,
He miss'd him, as home from his calling
    With thrice weary bones he would wend.

"No more would his heavy step lighten,
    No more would his hazel eyes glow,
No more would his smutty face brighten
    At sight of the darling. Ah, no!

"He lived by my bodings unharried,
    But when from his vision and mine,
Away the sweet lisper was carried,
    He pined, and long after would pine.

"Ay, truly.—And reason.—The sonsy—
    The bairn with his hair bright and curled,
He still had appeared to our fancy,
    The bonniest bairn in the world.

"As ruddy was he as a cherry,
    With dimple on chin and on cheek;
And never another as merry
    Was seen to play hide-and-go-seek.

BEREAVED. 31

"He, yet with his fun and affection,
 His canny bit pranks and his grace,
He wheedled my heart from dejection,
 And put a bright look on my face.

" Full oft upon one leg advancing,
 Across to the door he would go,
Wheel round on his heel, then go dancing
 With hop after hop down the row.

" When—Let my hand go!—When he perish'd,
 The rest were a balm to my woe:
But now, what remains to be cherish'd?
 But now, what remains to me now?

" Barely cold was the pet ere affected
 By fever they lay one and all;
But lay not like others neglected;
 I slept not to be at their call.

" Day and night, night and day without slumber,
 I watched till a-weary and worn;—
When Death took the gem of the number,
 I'd barely strength left me to mourn.

" I've mourn'd enough since. And tho' cruel
 Mishap like a curs'd hag would find
Her way to my door still, the jewel
 Has seldom been out of my mind.

"Another so light and so airy
  Ne'er gladden'd a fond mother's sight —
I oft heard her called a wee fairy,
  And heard her so called with delight.

"Whilst others played, by me she tarried,
  —The cherub!—and rumour avers
That now-a-days many are married,
  With not half the sense that was hers.

"A-down on the hearth-rug a-sitting
  The long winter nights she was heard,
The while her sweet fingers were knitting,
  To lilt out her lay like a bird.

"Did I appear cross! To me stealing,
  Askance in my face she would keek,
At which, e'er the victim of feeling,
  I could not but pat her bit cheek.

"She once, when I'd pricked this hard finger—
  No, he who in grave-clothes first slept—
—No, she—with the senses that linger
  I cannot tell which of them—wept.

"She vanished at last. Ah, an ocean
  Of trouble appeared that black cup;
But what was it all to the potion
  I now am commanded to sup?

BEREAVED.

"My husband, my bairnies, my blossoms!
—Well—well, I am wicked—yes, yes;
But take my loss home to your bosoms,
 And say if your sin would be less?

"My husband, my bairnies, my blossoms!
 Well—well,—I'll not murmur, but still
The anguish that teareth the bosom's
 Not, not to be bridled at will.

"The dear ones to perish so sudden!
 —'Twas only last night, by the hearth,
While I sat and mended their dudden,
 The bairnies were giddy with mirth.

"Their cousin came in, and they hasten'd
 To hand her, and, handing the chair,
The strings of her apron unfasten'd,
 And slipt the back comb from her hair.

"On leaving, the lassie discovered
 The prank they upon her had play'd;
Awhile hung her head, awhile hover'd,
 Then pinched both their noses and fled.

"They laugh'd, clapt their hands, and the father
 —Yea, I too, had laugh'd with the rest;
But something came o'er me which rather
 Brought sorrow than joy to my breast.

BEREAVED.

"The dear ones to perish so sudden—
  Last night of all nights by the hearth,
While I was a-mending their dudden,
  Why felt I no joy in their mirth?"

"The supper was set, and being over
  I help'd them to bed, and I think,
Once curl'd up aneath the green cover,
  They dover'd to sleep in a wink.

"I too laid me down, heart a-weary—
  And when the birds rose from their bed,
Somehow, by a dream dull and dreary,
  My eyes were fast lock'd in my head.

"Aroused by their voices, and yearning
  To kiss them, I sprang to the floor;
They kissed me, and bade me 'good morning,'
  Then whistled away from the door.

"Long after away they had hurried,
  Their music a-rang in my ears;
Then thought I of those we had buried,
  And thought of the jewels with tears.

"Then thought I—What said I?—Thus thinking
  Was I, when rat-tat went the pane,
And back into sense again shrinking,
  I into bed stumbled again.

"Did I sleep? I did weep. To his calling
  The father had gone hours before,
And now in that havoc appalling,
  He lies with the blossoms I bore.

"Did I sleep? I did weep. Heart a-weary,
  How oft have I so wept before—
I wept, and to weep, lone and dreary
  I've wandered the broken brick floor.

"Did I sleep? Well, your kind arm and steady
  My tottering steps, and now you
Go, get out the winding-sheets ready,
  And do what remaineth to do.

"Spread winding-sheets—one for the father,
  And two for the darlings, our pride,—
And one for the wife and the mother,
  Ah, soundly she'll sleep by their side!"

THE WILTED LEAF.

WILTED is the leaf, and blown
By the cold wind up and down,
That beheld thy promise fair,
Maiden with the dark brown hair!

Shatter'd is this heart, and hurl'd
By its grief-storm thro' the world,
Since it won that promise rare,
Maiden with the dark-brown hair!

Go thy ways! thy locks unbraid!
Thou hast but thyself betray'd,
And must e'en my pity share,
Maiden with the dark-brown hair!

DORA DEE.

There's not a may in Ellerton
By half so sweet to look upon—
In all the country round there's none
    So sweet as Dora Dee.

The blood-red rose to passer by,
May show with pride its precious dye;
There's not a bloom can charm the eye
    Like little Dora Dee.

The linnet's self its head may rear,
And pipe a note wild, sweet, and clear;
There's not a bird can charm the ear
    Like little Dora Dee.

The lady in yon castle grand,
May knees of noble lords command;
There's not a lady in the land
    The peer of Dora Dee.

THE LAD OF BEBSIDE.

My heart is away with the lad of Bebside,
And never can I to another be tied ;
Not, not to be titled a lord's wedded bride,
Could Jinny abandon the lad of Bebside.

He dances so clever, he whistles so fine,
He's flattered and wooed from the Blyth to the Tyne,
Yet spite of the proffers he meets far and wide,
I'm alone the beloved of the lad of Bebside.

He entered our door on the eve of the Fair,
And cracked with our folk in a manner so rare,
Next morning right early with spleen I was eyed
To link to the Fair with the lad of Bebside.

Last night at the dancing, 'mid scores of fine queans,
The eldest among them just out of her teens,
He chose me, and truly with pleasure and pride
I footed the jig with the lad of Bebside.

To wed me he's promised, and who can believe
A laddie like him can a lassie deceive ?
The moon's on the wane—ere another be spied,
I'll lie in the arms of the lad of Bebside.

MEG GOLDLOCKS.

Ye've heard of Meg Goldlocks of Willington Dene ?
The stoniest damsel that ever was seen ;
Yet, her beauty distress'd, with its splendour, the rest
Of the lasses for miles around Willington Dene.

Meek Mary of Howdon, with Robin would rove !
But once to the Dene should his roguish feet move,
A-jealous of Meg's unmatched beauty, her tongue
Was turned to a bell, and a merry peal rung.

Blithe Betsy of Percy, eyed Jim like a spy,
Lest o'er to the Dene he should slip on the sly ;
Nay, did she but dream it, with heart like to break,
She scowled when she met him for all the next week.

Sweet Nancy of Benton, deemed Willie her own,
Till he went to the Dene on an errand unknown ;
The errand to her was apparent as day,
And the rose on her dimpled cheek withered away.

Thus matters went on around Willington Dene,
Till East came a gallant and married the quean ;
That moment the rest of the lasses were blest,
And their lovers allowed to tread Willington Dene !

POOR ROSE.

"Beware! yon bird now in glee on the bough
    May drop into a snare : "
So sung we when a day of the past had passed away
    But not when Alf. was near.

Not Cilla, not I, nor Bessy need sigh,
    That ever he came this way ;
But a worthier far than Cilla and her
    Hath rued that evil day.

That hour the dire ban of Rosa began,
    When Alf. glode over the hill,
And hailed us each with a blink did reach
    And make our heart-strings thrill.

At the brook we'd stoop'd, and the water scoop'd,
    Our clean green pails into,
When a coal black rook beclouded the brook
    And away o'er the hill-top flew.

We startled, raised our heads and gazed—
    And ere the bird had swept
From sight, heart-light, with his blink so bright,
    The youth the waters leapt.

I felt his spell, and Bessy as well,
  As in her heart she knows ;
But Rose—did she look at her face in the brook,
  Or why in the brook look'd Rose ?

The fact was bared, when the bird ensnared,
  Was the village talk indeed ;
But he, the youth, had the look of truth—
  And who the heart can read ?

No Cilla ; no—not—even so—
  Not Bessy more than Cill,
Tho' she tost her head in pride, and said
  What Rose remembers still.

" I think of the glance that made your hearts dance ;
  But ever I think also
Of the grim black rook that darkened the brook,
  And away o'er the hill did go."

" Nay, Bessy, nay—and forbear, I pray,
  By any cold remark,
To deepen the shade that hangs o'er her head,
  If Rosa's weird be dark.

" 'The wilyest bird, on hedge ever heard '—
  Ah, well you know the rest ;
The stranger youth had the look of truth—
  And looks deceive the best.

"If love-mad driven poor Rose hath given,
    What to give is woe to her,
Another more wild had been beguiled
    By lures less dazzling far."

At my sharp reply did a fierce red dye
    Bemantle Bessy's cheek,
While Rose turned as pale as the moon o'er the dale,
    But never a word did speak.

With a downcast look her needles she took,
    Till off our neighbour went,
When my hand she took and gave me a look,
    Which worlds of meaning meant.

Her tears out-gushed—in my arms she rushed,
    And kissed her Cilla, and said
What never shall pass these lips till the grass
    Is green above my head.

But oft since then, and ever when
    I think of Rose and her ban,
Will the sad, sad strain awake in my brain,
    By which this ditty began.

"Beware! yon bird now in glee on the bough
    May drop into a snare!"
Alas, even so will the old thing go,
    But when will the best beware?

ROSA REA.

The following was suggested by a sweet little lyric, entitled "Resolution," translated from the German of Uhland.

THE sun is in the western sky
    And thro' the barley, she—
Comes she, the apple of my eye,
    The rose-cheeked Rosa Rea.

Away I slink the maid to meet,
    As if I went away,
Alone to please a pair of feet
    Resolved to go astray.

I whistle as I go, tho' what
    I cannot tell, but know
Right well my heart goes pit-a-pat
    With every note I blow.

Anon, I, silent as the path.
    Whereon I tread become,
The power to blow my whistle, hath
    Ta'en wing and left me dumb.

The lark's loud lilt so bright and clear
    Is ringing in the sky;
A dearer tune I hear—I hear
    Two little feet draw nigh.

Two feet I hear approaching near
  —Abashed I hing my head—
Two little feet a hornpipe beat,
  Or is't my heart instead?

A floweret I of scarlet dye
  Espy as on I tread;
The maid who trips this way hath lips—
  Two lips of richer red.

A floweret I hard by espy,
  A gem of azure hue;
The maid who hies this way hath eyes—
  Two eyes of sweeter blue.

Those tiny blooms my heart might steal,
  Did not a spell profound
Now gar my mortal reason reel,
  Or gar the world go round.

My senses swim, my sight grows dim,
  A-near, more near her tread—
Her little feet a hornpipe beat,
  Or is't my heart instead?

Ah, am I moving on my feet?
  Or am I on my head?
Do airy dreams my senses cheat?
  Am I alive or dead?

UNDECEIVED.

Not dead ! away, that notion, nay,
    Not in a dream I move ;
Lo, in the clear bright pool I near
    I see my own dear love.

She nears—appears a blink uprears
    My head—O joy !—ah see !
Till night's o'erhead, locked hand in hand
    Stand I, and—Rosa Rea !

UNDECEIVED.

SECURE within his citadel, my heart,
A roystering King, has quaft his goblets brimm'd
At pleasure's sparkling fount,—has quaft and slept
Has hugg'd the phantom of delight—and slept
Not dreaming from his sleep he'd e'er awake
To find his towers a ruin, and his bliss
Sepulchred in the dust : but now, alas !
The truth discover'd, he assumes his staff
And walks the world, and when he'd halt, lest
Should build another citadel, and play
The merry fool he played—a voice exclaims :
" Reflect !—the Earthquake ! " and he halteth not.

THE THREE MAIDENS.

A KNIGHT right bold rode over the wold,
    Saluted maidens three:
"Now, if each possess'd what she liked best,
    What would her portion be?"

The eldest replied: "A carriage of pride,
    And milkwhite steeds so fine,
With a prince of renown to claim as my own,
    And rapture unpeered were mine."

The second replied: "For no carriage of pride,
    Nor milkwhite steeds, I yearn;
But to move in the ball, the envy of all,
    And laugh the gallants to scorn."

The youngest she sighed, and shyly replied:
    "The sole, sole wish of my breast,
Is to merit the hand of the best in the land,
    And serve my husband the best."

Now alights from his steed the knight, and with speed
    He takes the shy maid by the hand;—
They mount and they ride—she's now the King's bride,
    And Queen of all the land.

THE BREEZELET.

CRIED Ciss to the breeze, as under the trees,
    She lay at her ease, one day,
"From thy rovings cease, and a maiden to please,
    Of thy doings breeze now say !

" Be it so," sang he ; " from the west I be,
    And where-ever in glee I rove,
In lane or on lea, with the blooms I'm free,
    And they—ever me—they love.

" The primrose that well may fear when the fell,
    Fierce north winds yell, I seek,
When lured by my spell, she peers from her cell,
    And a smile gilds the dell-pet's cheek.

" The violet meek in her velvet sleek,
    In love with the freak, alway,
To my fancy weak appeareth to seek,
    When I play with her cheek, more play.

" The daisy a-drest in her blood-laced vest,
    In her deep green nest, I know,
When her lips I've prest, with a pleasure blest,
    Is her little breast a glow.

"The glad daffodil oft dances her fill,
　As under the hill glide I,
And her pearly tears spill down into the rill,
　And yet with a trill leaps by.

"See, a fairy bold, her vesture of gold,
　The crocus unfold, in mirth,
And glories untold, where I've kist the mold,
　Illumine the cold, cold earth."

Thus sang the breeze a maiden to please,
　And Ciss in the trees, that night,
To rapture a prey sang Robin the lay,
　When a kiss did the may requite.

THE FATAL ERRAND.

My mother bade me go. I went:
　But beat my heart, ere I returned,
A rat-tat-tan, and what it meant
　Too soon I to my sorrow learned.

Her errand to the youth I ran,
　But had she me some other bade,
I had not felt that rat-tat-tan,
　Nor wept to think I ever had.

THE RING.

'Tis dead of night. Within a cloud
    The blood-red moon half shrouded lies;
A comet flares above; aloud
    " Tu-whit, tu-whoo ! " the owlet cries.

In such an hour in yonder tower,
    Why doth Britannia's Queen and pride
A vigil keep? To sigh and weep
    For one who at the block hath died.

" O Essex, oh, my joy and woe
    Did on thy joy and love depend;
And, Essex, I was doomed to sigh
    That day which saw thy dismal end.

" The ring I gave in moments fled,
    Had'st thou to me that ring but sent,
Thy precious blood had not been shed,
    These bosom chords had not been rent.

" But thou would'st die, and I must sigh,
    Tho' slander dogs the heels of fame,
And would deny the fact that I
    Could ever feel affection's flame.

"They say I'm proud, tho' not aloud—
 It's spoken in a bitter tone;
Tho' not aloud, they say I'm proud,
 And that my heart's a heart of stone.

"Ah, could the world the veil up-lift—
 These tinsel trappings—and survey
My soul on storm-tost seas adrift,
 How would they start at the display?

"My tenderness has not come short
 Of hers whose tears had thawed the churl;
I've been the dupe, if not the sport,
 Of passions worthy of a girl.

"And he on whom my hope was built,
 Ah, even he, a cruel act!—
Immersed me in a sea of guilt,
 Then left me with a bosom rack'd.

"How could his pride the block have dyed
 With his own crimson drops, before
To me he'd yield, to me his shield,
 From faction's fangs in the days of yore.

"How could—but was't his pride so vast
 Upon himself the blow that dealt?
In agony what if I sigh
 For one who mocked the touch I felt?

THE RING.

"For one who scorned the royal ire?
  Despised the feelings of this breast?
Possess'd me with a base desire
  To make of me a brothel jest?

"Awake, my soul! exert thy power;
  Another mine terrific sprung,
Take up thy burden, and this hour
  Be, be it into Lethe flung.

"Awake, and—oh!"—thus did she sigh—
  "Thou cruel Essex!"—when her ears
Are startled by a din, and by
  Her side a troubled dame appears.

"The Lady Nottingham to-night—
  This hour—upon her death-bed lies,
And lying in this woeful plight,
  'Go, bring the Monarch!' raves and cries.

"A secret rankles in her soul,
  The which she seems right fain to speak;
But when she tries, her eye-balls roll,
  And heavy sighs the sentence break."

For coach and steed at this with speed
  The Monarch calls in reason's spite,
And Queen, and guard, and coach and steed,
  Soon hurry thro' the vault of night.

THE RING.

Away they dart, the fleetful hart
  Not fleeter from the hounds away!
From bush and tree the small birds flee,
  One strikes the driver, in dismay.

O'er hills they hie, thro' dales that lie
  In shadows deep, they onward dash;
Where at the beat of steel-shod feet
  Live sparks from out the pebbles flash.

The clang, crash, squeal of hoof and wheel,
  The shriek of birdie in despair,
Their echoes wake or blend and make
  Dire music on the midnight air.

Tho' dire it be as on they flee,
  Our riders heed it not. One thought,
But one they know, and that is how
  They best may win the goal sought.

The groom's "whohoa" the ward's "holoa,"
  Are heard now in yon hall, wherein
In woeful wise a lady dies,
  And she—she moveth at the din.

Yet mark not this a trusty band,
  Who with o'er-burden'd feeling watch
That moment when death's cold, cold hand
  Shall life from her endearments snatch.

In truth the tear bedims their sight,
  And had conceal'd the fact, had they
Possessed a light more pure and bright
  Than what their sickly lamps display.

Too, man's but man; and how-be-it
  The spirit would her task fulfil,
The senses weary and remit
  Their aptness to obey the will.

Three nights have vanished since her end
  Appear'd but on the threshold; lo!
A bitter thing to see a friend
  Thus struggling with the common foe.

So feel they, muse they, cry "Ah, me!"
  Or whisper low, or shake the head,
When nears the mighty Queen, and see!
  The dying riseth on her bed.

The band that ties her hair unties,
  Her hair a-down her shoulders strays;
A gleam re-lights her sunken eyes,
  And o'er her ghastly features plays.

"Well thou art here," she gasps, "and well
  With death I've striven to reveal
What, what it racks my soul to tell,
  And doubly racks it to conceal.

"When he who late for treason bled,
  Had let the Spanish feel his sword,
The fame on which his spirit fed,
  Was it not graced by your regard?

"Then gave you not to him a ring,
  Averring 'If at any time
Thou shalt my frown upon thee bring,
  Show that and I'll forgive the crime?'

"He took that ring, the period came
  When he did need its magic might;
He gave it me to give—my shame!—
  It never met his monarch's sight.

"My lord to Essex being a foe,
  Prevailed on me to keep the boon;
The rest is known."—A moment, now,
  Her majesty is turned to stone.

Her late flushed cheeks are bleak and blanched,
  Her eyes shoot forth a frantic glare;
Her lips are writhed, her hands are clenched,
  And in their grasp her up-torn hair.

"Hell and damnation eat thee up—
  The seven vials the prophet saw
Be thine," at last she cried, "to sup
  For this base breach of human law.

"Great God, protect me, I am mad—
   This trial is too much for one
With might until this moment clad
   To trample death and terror down.

"Kingdoms have trembled at my frown,
   Or at my smile have danced for joy;
But now the star of glory's flown,
   That shone upon the hours gone by.

"Ah, never more! ah, never more
   Will joy, will peace to me return!"
This said, she sank upon the floor,
   And there remained her woes to mourn.

Nor could she be consoled, nor would,
   But rather nursed her mind's distress;
Till sorrow gave her to her shroud,
   And thus did end the Good Queen Bess.

STANZAS.

The hopes that allured me
To cope with the worst,
At length have secured me
The tortures accurst,
Of fever and grief,
And frenzy—in brief
Ills—ills from which Death is the only relief.

But Titan-like lieth
My soul in her chains—
Hourly she sigheth,
The answer she gains,
But adds night and day
To pain and dismay—
'Tis the scream of the vulture despair at his prey.

LO, THE DAY.

Lo the day begins to rise,
    And the shadows of the night,
Overtaken with surprise,
    Blushing fly his presence bright;
Cease thy briny tears to flow,
    Not another murmur sigh;
Thine hath been the cup of woe,
    Now be thine the cup of joy.

Wakened by the voice of morn,
    See, the little urchin Mirth,
How she, laughing Care to scorn,
    Skippeth o'er the jocund earth;
Don, O, don thy best attire,
    Snatch, O, snatch this balm to pain,
Ere the beams of day retire,
    And thy night sets in again.

THE HELL BROTH.

The devil and the devil's brood
   Around a boiling cauldron hung,
While in a nook in merry mood
   Grim Death a dainty ditty sung;
For guided by a baleful star
   The devil himself had caused to beam,
Lo, myriads hurried from afar
   To reap the fruit of a darksome dream:
On, on they came with cheek a-flame
   And lips that quivered as they sought
In tones subdued the demon brood,
   For but a drop of the magic pot.
—Anon around was the hell-broth spun,
   And a measure brimmed to old and young,
The while delighted with the fun,
   Grim Death a merry ditty sung.

That potion quaft in his conceit,
   Behold the dwarf a giant tread,
At least a hundred thousand feet
   Above his worthier neighbour's head;
Despising still or lord or serf,
   About the land he strutting goes,
'Till bang against a brother dwarf,
   The merry fellow runs his nose:

THE HELL BROTH.

Thus many a one—loon, fop, and clown—
  A lesson to their sorrow got,
And yet aloud they pray the brood
  For deeper draughts of the magic pot.
—Anon around was the hell-broth spun,
  And a measure drained by old and young,
The while delighted with the fun,
  Grim Death a merry ditty sung.

New double-drugg'd the rout about
  A soul-consuming furnace bore,
And what they took to put it out,
  But only made it burn the more:
It burnt in heart, it burnt in brain,
  And from its fumes arose a sprite,
One, whom her favours to obtain
  They chased by day, they chased by night;
And still as they deemed her their prey,
  Away, away with a leer she shot,
'Mid cries right loud to the demon brood,
  For deeper draughts of the magic pot.
—Again around was the hell-broth spun,
  And a measure drained by old and young,
The while delighted with the fun,
  Grim Death a merry ditty sung.

So la, ta, la!—that fiery draught
  Now led them one and all a dance:
Lo, ere the drug was wholly quaft,
  Each threw on each a lurid glance;

And from that glance a wasp took wing,
  From busy tongue to ear it flew,
And ever around it bore a sting
  The devil himself had cause to rue :
It stung them black, it stung them blue,
  And with each sting the louder got,
Their cries right loud to the demon brood,
  For deeper draughts of the magic pot.
—Again around was the hell-broth spun,
  And a measure drained by old and young,
The while delighted with the fun,
  Grim Death a merrier ditty sung.

That horrid draught being duly quaft,
  A cry o'er plain and mountain rolled,
At which the strong the weaker took,
  And bartered body and soul for gold :
And of the gold thus gotten, they
  At once a gloomy castle built,
Whose dome might from the eye of day
  Forever hide their horrid guilt :
Tombed in their victims' blood-price thus,
  Long revelled they and faltered not
To cry aloud to the demon brood,
  For deeper draughts of the magic pot.
—But around no more was the hell-broth spun ;
  Awe-stuck the fiends in the pot had sprung,
The while surfeited with the fun,
  Death cursed the merry lay he'd sung.

THE REIGN OF GOLD.

It sounded in castle and palace,
 It sounded in cottage and shed,
It sped over mountains and valleys,
 And withered the earth as it sped ;
Like a blast in its fell consummation
 Of all that we holy should hold,
Thrilled, thrilled thro' the nerves of the nation,
 A cry for the reign of King Gold.

Upstarted the chiefs of the city,
 And sending it back with a ring,
To the air of a popular ditty,
 Erected a throne to the king:
'Twas based upon fiendish persuasions,
 Cemented by crimes manifold:
Embellished by specious ovations,
 That dazzled the foes of King Gold.

The prey of unruly emotion,
 The miner and diver go forth,
And the depths of the earth and the ocean
 Are shorn of their lustre and worth ;
The mountain is riven asunder,
 The days of the valley are told ;
And sinew, and glory, and grandeur,
 Are sapped for a smile of King Gold.

THE REIGN OF GOLD.

Beguiled of their native demeanour,
  The high rush with heirlooms and bays;
The poor with what gold cannot weigh, nor
  The skill of the pedant appraise;
The soldier he spurs with his duty,
  And lo! by the frenzy made bold,
The damsel she glides with her beauty,
  To garnish the brow of King Gold.

Accustomed to traffic forbidden
  By honour—by heaven—each hour,
The purest, by conscience unchidden,
  Laugh, laugh at the noble and pure;
And Chastity, rein'd in a halter,
  Is led to the temple and sold,—
Devotion herself, at the altar,
  Yields homage alone to King Gold.

Affection, on whose honey blossom,
  The child of affliction still fed—
Affection is plucked from the bosom,
  And malice implanted instead;
And dark grow the brows of the tender,
  And colder the hearts of the cold:—
Love, pity, and justice surrender
  Their charge to the hounds of King Gold.

See, see, from the scar'd earth ascending,
  A cloud o'er the welkin expands;
See, see, 'mid the dense vapour bending,
  Pale women with uplifted hands;

THE REIGN OF GOLD.

Smokes thus to the bridegroom of Circe,
 The dear blood of hundreds untold;
Invokes thus the angel of mercy
 A curse on the reign of King Gold.

It sounded in castle and palace,
 It sounded in cottage and shed,
It sped over mountains and valleys,
 And withered the earth as it sped;
Like a blast in its fell consummation
 Of all that we holy should hold,
Thrilled, thrilled thro' the nerves of the nation;
 "Cling! clang! for the reign of King Gold."

DAFFODIL AND DAISY.

Deck'd in a many gems of morn,
 A daffodil without a peer,
I reared my head, and treat with scorn
 A one-pearl-gifted daisy near.

That very hour, lo! wind-a-rock'd
 Was I left gemless evermore;
Nay, made to envy what I'd mock'd,
 That one sweet pearl the daisy wore.

A LULLABY.

(*Suggested by an old verse.*)

Thro' the dark and dreary night,
　Golden slumbers kiss thine eyes;
Sleep, and in the early light
　With a golden smile arise!
　　Sleep, my baby, do not cry
　　—Lulla, lulla, lullaby.

Trouble art thou? baby nay;
　Brightest star in all my sky,
Since was turned to night my day,
　And thy father—Do not cry!
　　Sleep, my baby, do not cry
　　—Lulla, lulla, lullaby.

The round red moon, she's sinking low,
　The wind up-tears the very roof;—
The moon may sink, the wind may blow,
　For thee, my child, I'm tempest proof.
　　Sleep, my baby, do not cry
　　—Lulla, lulla, lullaby.

THE COLLIER LAD.

My lad he is a Collier Lad,
    And ere the lark awakes,
He's up and away to spend the day
    Where daylight never breaks;
But when at last the day has pass'd,
    Clean washed and cleanly clad,
He courts his Nell who loveth well
    Her handsome Collier Lad.

Chorus—There's not his match in smoky Shields;
    Newcastle never had
A lad more tight, nor trim, nor bright
    Than is my Collier Lad.

Tho' doomed to labour under ground,
    A merry lad is he;
And when a holiday comes round,
    He'll spend that day in glee;
He'll tell his tale o'er a pint of ale,
    And crack his joke, and bad
Must be the heart who loveth not
    To hear the Collier Lad.

    Chorus—There's not his match, etc.

At bowling matches on the green
  He ever takes the lead,
For none can swing his arm and fling
  With such a pith and speed;
His bowl is seen to skim the green,
  And bound as if right glad
To hear the cry of victory
  Salute the Collier Lad.

  Chorus—There's not his match, etc.

When 'gainst the wall they play the ball,
  He's never known to lag,
But up and down he gars it bowne,
  Till all his rivals fag;
When deftly—lo! he strikes a blow
  Which gars them all look sad,
And wonder how it came to pass
  They play'd the Collier Lad.

  Chorus—There's not his match, etc.

The quoits are out, the hobs are fix'd,
  The first round quoit he flings
Enrings the hob; and lo! the next
  The hob again unrings;
And thus he'll play a summer day,
  The theme of those who gad;
And youngsters shrink to bet their brass
  Against the Collier Lad.

  Chorus—There's not his match, etc.

When in the dance he doth advance,
  The rest all sigh to see
How he can spring and kick his heels,
  When they a-wearied be ;
Your one-two-three, with either knee
  He'll beat, and then, glee mad,
A heel-o'er-head leap, crowns the dance
  Danced by the Collier Lad.

    Chorus—There's not his match, etc.

Besides a will and pith and skill,
  My laddie owns a heart
That never once would suffer him
  To act a cruel part ;
That to the poor would ope the door
  To share the last he had ;
And many a secret blessing's pour'd
  Upon my Collier Lad.

    Chorus—There's not his match, etc.

He seldom goes to church, I own,
  And when he does, why then,
He with a leer will sit and hear,
  And doubt the holy men ;
This very much annoys my heart ;
  But soon as we are wed,
To please the priest, I'll do my best
  To tame my Collier Lad.

    Chorus—There's not his match, etc.

THE SEATON TERRACE LASS.

My love at Seaton Terrace dwells,
    A hale and hearty wight,
Who lilts away the summer day,
    Also the winter night;
The merriest bird with rapture stirr'd,
    Could never yet surpass
The melody awaken'd by
    The Seaton Terrace lass!

Chorus.—Her like is not in hall or cot;
    And you would vainly pass
From Tweed to Wear for one to peer
    The Seaton Terrace lass.

She's graceful as a lily-wand,
    Right modest too is she,
And then ye'll search in vain the land
    To find a busier bee;
Like silver clear her iron gear,
    Like burnished gold, the brass—
For tidiness there's none to peer
    The Seaton Terrace lass.

    Chorus.—Her like is not, etc.

More restless than a clucking hen
    About her, Minnie stirs ;
"Go, jewel, knit your fancy net,
    And I will scour the floors."
" Enjoy the day, a-down the way
    Where greenest grows the grass ;
No help I need," replies with speed
    The Seaton Terrace lass.

    Chorus—Her like is not, etc.

She'll knit or sew, she'll bake or brew—
    She'll wash the clothes so clean,
The very daisy pales beside
    Her linen on the green ;
Then what she'll do, with ease she'll do,
    And still her manner has
A charm would gar a stoic woo
    The Seaton Terrace lass.

    Chorus—Her like is not, etc.

Discomfort flies her dark brown eyes,
    And when the men folk come
All black and weary from the pit,
    They find a welcome home :
Her brothers tease her, and a pride,
    The father feeleth as
Again he meets, again he greets
    The Seaton Terrace lass.

    Chorus—Her like is not, etc.

When day is past and night at last
  Begins to cloud the dell,
She'll take her skiel and out she'll steal,
  And meet me at the well;
Then, oh! how fleet the moments sweet—
  Yet fleeter shall they pass,
That night the Bebside laddie weds
  The Seaton Terrace lass.

Chorus—Her like is not in hall or cot,
    And vainly would you pass
    From Tweed to Wear for one to peer
    The Seaton Terrace lass.

WONDER-BOUND.

They'd told me he was hoar and old,
  They'd told me he was weak and worn,
And wonder-bound did I behold
  Him merry as a summer morn.

Bound, wonder-bound; but when I found
  Thine eyes upon his eyes had beam'd,
I only had been wonder-bound
  Had he to me less merry seem'd.

KIT CLARK.

MEG MILLER skipt over to Horton,
  And sang as she went like the lark ;
" A pair of bright eyes hath Tim Morton,
  Yet not his the blink of Kit Clark.

" Bob Harkas hath hair crisp and curly ;
  And when to his queer jokes, we hark,
Dour Doll even fails to look surly—
  Yet Bob cannot joke like Kit Clark.

" Bill Nichol can whistle so clearly,
  The dogs run around him and bark ;
And Nan likes to hear him right dearly—
  Yet Bill cannot pipe like Kit Clark.

"Tom Smith like a frantic one danceth
  As down the row comes he from wark ;
And Nell's tinder heart he entranceth—
  Yet Tom lacks the spring of Kit Clark.

" Jos Rutter—who dresses like Rutter ?
  The lad is a bit of a spark ;
He puts Bella's heart in a flutter—
  Yet Jos—what is Jos to Kit Clark ?

"Kit Clark is both handsome and clever,
  His eyes shine like stars in the dark ;
Has Cowpen his equal ?—no, never !
  Not one is a match for Kit Clark."

MY LOVED ONE.

My loved one appears
  In a vision by night,
The loveliest jewel
  Ever gladdened the sight;
With her pensive blue eyes,
  And her forehead, downcast,
She comes to relieve
  My racked bosom at last:
Anon upon Love's
  Golden pinions I fly,
And my arms are outstretched
  To encompass my joy;
But ere she's embraced,
  I awake—and awake,
My heart the day long—
  Oh my heart's like to break !

THE SEER.

Would I could waken numbers, brighter, sweeter,
    Than is the lark's song in the cloud above,
Then would I tell you in befitting metre,
    How much the Seer is worthy of your love.

Shy, sensitive is he, and far from equal
    Unto the battle of material life,
He strives unheeded and, too oft the sequel,
    Unheeded falleth in the bitter strife.

Averse to falsehood and pretences hollow,
    Averse to slander, cruelty, and wrong,
He scorns the gilded car of pomp to follow,
    And underneath is trampled by the throng.

Too nobly strung of self to brook the mention—
    Too sweetly strung to give another pain—
Too finely strung to pleasure in contention,
    He seeks within the meed he would obtain.

Unlike the crowd who never dare look inward,
    Lest they a hideous spectre there should meet,
Would point to secret longings prompting sinward,
    He looks within and finds a solace sweet.

Ay, in a conscience pure he sees a charmer—
    A harper from whose harp such tones are hurl'd,
They act as mighty spells, as tested armour,
    To shield him from the malice of the world.

"Go on, brave heart," he hears an anthem chanted,
    The distant echoes of that harp's weird tones;
"Go on—to thee a richer dower is granted
    Than that which gilds a hundred monarchs' thrones.

"Thou may'st be thrust aside and scorned and taunted
    As being a lunatic, a knave or fool,
Thou hast within thy inner being planted
    A power that yet shall put the world to school.

"Thou may'st be destined here to tribulation;
    Thy every pang shall prove a key, by which,
Thou shalt unlock some safe of the Creation,
    And with its precious stores thy mind enrich.

"Illumined by that sun forever burning,
    Deep in the centre of the inner spheres,
Thou shalt be gifted with the gift of learning
    What lieth hidden from thy mortal peers.

"In every planet in the midnight heaven—
    In every hue doth in the rainbow blend,
Shalt thou perceive a lore and meaning, given
    To very few on earth to comprehend.

"The very flower upon the meadow blowing—
The very weed down trampled on the road,
Shall be to thee a priceless casquet, glowing
With glories hinting of the light of God.

"In every breezelet—nay, in the commotion
Of raging winds—in every streamlet clear—
Nay, in the roaring of the mighty ocean,
Shalt thou hear sounds will gladden thee to hear.

"Thus shalt thou in the Universe external,
The Universe internal read, and so
Possess what shall be to the weal eternal
Of earth's benighted 'habitants to know.

"The buried eons of the Past—their history,
Still glows in characters that thou shalt read;
And from the future thou shalt pluck its mystery,
And point the goal to where the moments lead.

"Whatever thrills the heart with feelings precious,
Whatever tends to cast the spirit down,
The deed delightful, or the hint pernicious,
Shall claim withal in turn thy smile or frown.

"Remind shalt thou the soul aweary, weary
Even with the battle thou thyself hast fought,
How thro' deep failure and thro' toil uncheery,
Must every triumph worth his care be wrought.

"Nay even at the hest of a volition
  Still, still to highest purposes attuned,
Shalt thou go forth a monarch, and ambition
  And evils many with thy glance confound.

"'Woe,' black-browed guilt shall cry ; and 'woe' and
    vanish
  Despair and desolation, sisters sad ;
And for the hydra-brood thou thus shalt banish,
  Celestial Love shall make the spirit glad.

"Uplifting them by slow yet sure gradations,
  From spheres inferne into the spheres superne,
Shalt thou thus prove a boon unto the nations,
  And in return a boon divine shalt earn.

"If not in monuments of brass or marble,
  Deep in men's spirits shall thy glory glow ;
And little ones shall of the wonders warble
  Accomplished by the wise man long ago.

"All this and more than this shall be thy guerdon,—
  The sense of having acted right!"—So says
The happy echo of that harp's sweet burden
  A certain Seraph in his bosom plays.

And this enableth the true seer ever
  To triumph tho' he falleth, and to pray
That theirs like his may be a portion, never,
  Who plot and plan to take his life away.

Ah, to the last his words and deeds are sweeter
  Than is the lark's song in the cloud above,
And rare the bard could find befitting metre,
  To hymn the love we owe this child of Love!

TIT-FOR-TAT.

"Say, whither goes my buxom maid
  All with the coal-black e'e?"
"Before I answer that," she said,
  "Give ear, and answer me.

"Pray, hast thou e'er thy counsel kept?"
  "Ay, and still can," said he:
"And so can I," said she, and swept
  A-lilting o'er the lea.

ANNIE.

Coal black are the tresses of Fanny,
    But never a mortal could see
The coal-coloured tresses of Annie,
    And be as a body should be.

White, white, is her forehead, and bonnie—
    And when she goes down to the well,
The beat of the footstep of Annie,
    The wrath of a tiger would quell.

Red, red, are her round cheeks and bonnie—
    And when she is knitting, her tone—
The charm of the accents of Annie,
    Would ravish the heart of a stone.

Nay, rare are her graces and many,
    But nothing whatever can be
Compared to the sweet glance of Annie,—
    The glance she has given to me.

AWAY TO THE WELL.

Away to the well lilted Annie—
  Away with her skiel to the well;
Away to the well whistled Johnnie,
  The pride and delight of the dell.

Sweet, sweet is the well; but ah, sweeter,
  The words of the silver-tongued elf;
And I counsel the youth who shall meet her,
  To keep a strict guard on himself.

Deep, deep is the well; but ah, deeper,
  The guile of the silver-tongued elf;
And the laugher she'll turn to a weeper,
  Unless he look well to himself.

'Twas thus proved the mortal to Johnnie:
  Lo, pale, now, he wanders the dell,—
Pale, pale with the potion that Annie
  Had caused him to drink at the well.

SYMPATHY.

In despite of the cold and the gloom,
To ornament summer's bleak tomb,
  Blooms the snowdrop ; and lo ! at the sight,
  Sad Flora is thrilled with delight,
And exults in the moments to come.

In despite of the sneers of the proud,
To garnish my hope's ebon shroud,
  Glows thy tear-drop ; and lo ! I'm possessed
  Of Flora's rich feelings, when blest
With the sight of the first of her brood.

But once having granted my fill
Of sympathy's heart-cheering rill,—
  Beloved ! refrain ; it were base,
  To sweep yon sweet rose from its vase
That the thistle might blossom at will.

NANNY TO BESSY.

ELEVEN long winters departed
  Since you and he sailed o'er the main?
Dear, dear—I've been thrice broken-hearted,
  And thrice—but, ah, let me refrain.—

There was not a lassie in Plessy,
  Nay, truly there was not a lad,
That morning you left us all, Bessy,
  But dropped a kind tear and look'd sad.

A week ere ye went ye were married—
  Yes, yes, I remember aright;
The lads and the lasses all hurried
  To dance at your bridals that night.

With others, were Mary from Horton,
  And Harry from over the fields;
Your prim cousin Peggy from Chirton,
  And diddler Allen from Shields.

Piper Tom, with his pipes in the corner,
  Did pipe till the red morn a-broke;
And we danced and we sung in our turn, or
  Gave vent to our glee in a joke.

NANNY TO BESSY.

That seems but last night, tho' eleven
    Black winters have flown since, and yet
Ye're bright as yon star in the heaven,
    Whilst I—but I winnot regret.

Ye're just bright and fresh and as rosy
    As when ye last left us all, just;
Whilst 1 am a poor wither'd posy
    The passer has strampt in the dust.

This was not so always; no, clearly
    —When lasses—the burnie has shown
The rose on your dimpled cheek nearly
    Out-matched by the rose on my own.

Twinn'd sisters appeared we, and canny
    Together we'd link o'er the wold,
When Bessy's bit secrets to Nanny,
    And Nanny's to Bessy were told.

Nay's one, we grew up until Harry
    Was mine—but, was mine for how long?
Then, the changes that followed,—the worry,
    The guilt, and the shame, and the wrong?

—Ye knew my 'curst bane and besetter?
    Brown? Piers with the thievish black e'e?
He danced at your wedding, and better
    Than any but Harry danced he.

The sight sent the lasses a-skarling,
  Whenever he came into view;
And many a fond mother's darling
  Has lived his deception to rue.

Meg Wilson, a-down the green loaning,
  Skipped with him a fine afternoon;
When last she went there she was moaning,
  Her heart like a harp out of tune.

Even Cary, the dour-looking donnet,
  Who'd looked on my downfall with scorn,
Was smit with his blink, and her bonnet
  One Monday was found in the corn.

Nay, many with him tripped and tumbled
  As I'd tripped and tumbled—what then?
Not one by her fall was so humbled,
  Or put to one half of my pain.

When Harry was brought on a barrow,
  A corpse from the pit, had I known
—But Brown, who had long been his marrow,
  Then, who was so kind as Piers Brown?

He showed himself ready and willing
  To lighten the load I endured;
He gather'd me many a shilling,
  And whatso I needed procured.

The bones of my Harry right duly
  Were laid in the grave by his aid;
Then slipt he to see me—too truly
  So slipt till my pride was low laid.

There's many to point and to titter
  At one who has happen'd a fall—
And into the cup that is bitter,
  The petty still empty their gall.

There's many to point and to titter
  At one that has happened to fall—
And into my potion so bitter,
  The petty so emptied their gall.

Then mine was a hardship and trouble;
  When touch'd by deceit's magic mace,
My pride went away like a bubble,
  Then mine was a pitiful case.

Then deep on my check burn'd the scarlet,
  The token of sin and of shame;
And many did call me a harlot,
  More worthy than I of the name.

Then mishap to mishap, like billow
  To billow succeeded, and I
Was laid with my head on my pillow,
  And no one to solace me nigh.

Then perished the darlings you kindly
    Remember and ask for—alorn,
I lay by the morsels and blindly,
    Then cursed the dark hour I was born.

A-lorn by the dead lay I—driven
    To frenzy by grief, shame, and scorn,
And lifted my two hands to heaven,
    Then cursed the dark hour I was born.

I cursed—felt accursed—nay, that hourly
    I'd dogg'd by a black devil been ;
And he, when he'd speeded most surely,
    Had held in derision my teen.

He'd dazzled and led me to yamour,
    For baubles one ought to despise,
Then whipt from my vision the glamour,
    And shown the sad truth to my eyes.

He'd mounted the air, and a snelling
    Bleak blast had swept valley and plain,
And the dwelling of joy made the dwelling
    Of dire desolation and pain.

Years long the keen thought of the cruel
    Black lot of thy crony a-led
Her to feel, and to prate thus, and—jewel !—
    Yet puts a mill-wheel in her head.

The pale morning finds me a-wringing
　My hands for the dearies in vain;
The day passes by without bringing
　Me any relief to my pain.

Evermore on my heart feeds the canker,
　The cruel reflection that—ay—
That they for a morsel did hanker,
　I had not a penny to buy.

Overcome by despair in confusion
　Of mind, I will wander oft, when
The prey of a charming delusion,
　They seem to me living again.

Again on their hazels a-prancing,
　They hie as they hied o'er the way,
The midges above them a-dancing,
　Are not half so merry as they.

Again up and down the ball boundeth,
　A-tween their bit hands and the earth,
Till rapture their senses confoundeth,
　And laughter gives vent to their mirth.

Again—in my sight—my woe banished,—
　The birds seem a-living again,
Then quickly I find them a-vanished,
　And sorrow yet with me, and pain.

While yet but a lassie, I married ;
While yet in my teens I was left ;
Ere olden to frenzy was harried—
Ere olden of hope I'm a-reft.

A reed by the wild wind a-broken
Am I, and my tongue in vain seeks
To utter the tale which a-spoken,
Would hurry that rose from your cheeks.

But let me refrain. Since we parted—
Ah lass, since ye went o'er the main ;
Since then I've been thrice broken-hearted,
And thrice—but ah, let me refrain.

LOVE WITHOUT HOPE.

The glory of her charms I felt,
  And thro' my frame electric ran
What made my stubborn heart to melt,
  And feel as hearts of passion can;
And from that hour, her eyes of jet,
  And every trait and every hue,
In her delightful being met,
  Pursues me and shall e'er pursue.

A vision bright, a form of light,
  She glides before my inner eyes;
And tho' anear she doth appear,
  In vain for her my bosom sighs—
In vain, in vain, and woe and pain
  Are mine—and woe and pain alone—
Another's arms must fold those charms,
  Which I would give a world to own.

Upon the block with nerve of rock,
  This hour would see my head reclined,
Could this but show o'er all below
  My image in her heart were shrined;

LOVE WITHOUT HOPE.

Yes, yes, for this unequalled bliss,
  Upon the wings of rapture borne,
My soul would cleave the air and leave
  Her mortal bonds asunder torn!

A niche possessed within her breast,
  Ay, more than life I'd value that—
What were it then, could I but strain
  Her to my heart my own? ay, what?
Entranced I feel,—my senses reel,—
  Up in a fiery whirlwind caught
Away, fly they, and leave me—ay,
  Half frantic at the very thought!

What would I have, what do I crave?
  What were a sin for me to touch!—
Yon radiant star that beams from far,
  Her lustre equals twenty such;
She's past compare a jewel rare,
  Of value more than crowns can boast;
Whilst I who sigh—ah what am I?
  A wretch who merits scorn at most.

Far, far above my worth and love
  Is she—and were she less divine,
Another's arms would fold her charms,
  And I were destined still to pine;

Thus double doomed to be consumed
  By passion's raging fires, I know
On earth a hell as fierce and fell,
  As aught a future state could show.

Alas! alas! we seldom love
  Where love may equal love obtain;
Our idols in our fancy move—
  Fleet phantoms we may chase in vain;
We either love what's little worth,
  And live to rue the sequel; or,
What never can be ours on earth,
  And so must evermore deplore!

THE STARS ARE TWINKLING.

The stars are twinkling in the sky,
  As to the pit I go;
I think not of the sheen on high,
  But of the gloom below.

Not rest nor peace, but toil and strife,
  Do there the soul enthral;
And turn the precious cup of life
  Into a cup of gall.

THE QUESTION.

WHAT can he ail ? I hear them ask ;
   And what can make his cheek so pale ?
Ah, that to answer were a task
   For which no effort could avail,
To say I love were but to say
   What many another might as well,
Who never felt the cruel sway
   Which makes my heart with sorrow swell.

Dear are the pains of love and sweet,
   Yet he who loves, and loves in vain,
Endures a torment more complete
   Than any love unsweetened pain,
Nay, keener than the savage fangs,
   Which limb from limb their victim tear,
And much more cruel are the pangs
   Which drive a lover to despair.

With feelings racked, without a spark
   Of hope to give those feelings rest,
The darksome grave is not so dark
   As is the chaos in his breast :

THE QUESTION.

The brightest hour that comes and goes,
    Might just as well be dull as bright,
His grief o'er all a shadow throws,
    That hides the splendour from his sight.

Unmoved he eyes the sun arise,
    Yea, doth without a thrill behold
The sun down go at ev'ning, tho'
    He settles in a sea of gold :
The sweetest flower of field or bower,
    The brightest star by night revealed,
To him's not rare, nor sweet, nor fair,
    For him no joyous beam can yield.

The tempest swells and roars and yells,
    Up-tears and heaves to earth the oak ;
The death-bolts crash, the lightnings flash,
    And cities wrap in flame and smoke :
Let thunder crash, and lightnings flash,
    And bid him perish as they can ;
The storm he hears no death-dart bears,
    Like that which makes his life a ban.

O'er all he sees, o'er all he hears,
    The raven shades of woe are cast ;
And all his hopes, delights, and fears,
    Are now but phantoms of the past ;

The past, the present, future, ay
   To all he's dead and cold, except
The worm that eats the heart away,
   Wherein Peace long her vigils kept.

He wanders wide of human haunts,
   What others do he little recks;
Their very sympathy or taunts,
   Can little soothe, can little vex;
Where-e'er he moves, where-e'er he turns,
   One, but one image meets his ken;
For that he yearns and pines and mourns,
   And yearns and mourns for that in vain.

Away! away with questions, which
   No mortal yet could answer—nay,
My pangs are far beyond the pitch
   Of seraph-tongue or pen to say;
To speak of love were but to speak
   Of what another might, whose heart
Was never forced like mine to break,
   Yet while it breaks to hide the smart!

THE DANCE.

MET we in the festal hall,
  Met—our feelings blended !
Love alone shall lead the ball,
  Truth alone shall end it.

Wakes an air, and here and there,
  Soon the dance we tread, when
Ladies bright admire the knight,
  Gallant knights the maiden.

Here and there, an envied pair
  Mid the bright we shimmer ;
Cheer right rare responds to cheer,
  Brimmer clinks with brimmer.

Dance we still, and dance we till
  On our vision waneth
Every light that gilds the night,
  And love in triumph reigneth.

Praised by all we left the hall,
  But, within us ever,
Rapture's self still lead a ball
  Peace should end—ah ! never.

THE SPELL.

"Love's a pleasure, love's a treasure,
Why the joys of love withstand?"
Alf so pleadeth, Effie heedeth
And—What ails the lily-wand?

Lighter grow her airs and lighter—
Glances she would shun she seeks;
Brighter burn her eyes, and brighter
Burns the scarlet on her cheeks.

Leaps her heart within her; cheerly
Smiles the earth in silence girt;
Dance the stars above, and rarely,
All in concord with her heart.

Redder than the red rose blowing
Sinks she in her woer's arms;
Many a mad, mad vow avowing
Melt they in each other's charms.

For a season vanished reason—
Vanished to return and view
Loved and lover—doomed for ever—
Doom'd the spell of love to rue.

THE ANGEL MOTHER.

I HAD a vision of the dear departed,
    The while stone-dead to outer things I lay;
And " Go," she said—" and tell the broken-hearted,
    What now my will shall to thy mind convey.

" I've passed the portals I so often dreaded,
    And by the fiery trial unconsumed
I find myself to life, not death, yet wedded—
    Even I whose relics you beheld entombed.

" To me the baubles of the world have vanished,
    Even with the garments I behind have left;
But not one treasure from my heart is banished,
    Not of one golden hope am I bereft.

" The self-same soul am I, the self-same being
    In every human faculty the same,
Save with a clearer, keener sense of seeing
    What path to glory leads, and what to shame.

" The wife's devotion and affection tender,—
    The mother's sweet solicitude and all
That did our home a thing of beauty render,
    Is mine, or haunts me still, and ever shall.

"Even from my sphere beyond your sphere located
 I'm oft permitted to return—return!
To seek the halls my change left desolated,—
 To bless the dear ones left that change to mourn.

"I see the brave man by the hearth-stone sitting,
 To whom my being was and yet is wed,
I see the past before his vision flitting,—
 I see the tear-drops for his lost one shed.

"Not void of hope the dust he saw enshrouded,
 Itself was but a cerement to a soul,
Whose vision never could by death be clouded—
 He yet hath sorrows he may yet control.

"Full often o'er the welkin of his vision
 I see an ebon cloudlet stealing, when
A sigh is utter'd lest his hope, elysian,
 Is but a phantom of the minds of men.

"Upon my knees, unseen, before him kneeling
 I gaze into those eyes tear-blinded, till
A sense of sadness yieldeth to a feeling
 As sweet as ever did a bosom thrill.

"I point the images of those yet living,
 —Thus speak I still as I when with you spake—
When from the past into the present driven,
 His heart is up and toiling for their sake.

"'Even for my girl,' he cries, 'so bright and airy—
Even for my little boy just lisping, I
Must try this death-bell monotone to vary,
And on life's harp awake life's battle cry.'

"As he resolveth even so he doeth,
And all the little I can do, I do
To help him to the object he pursueth,
Or open vistas brighter to his view.

"I cannot wash as wont our jewels' faces,—
I cannot comb as wont their golden hair;
But I can lock them in my fond embraces,
And I can gild their minds with fancies rare.

"I cannot fetch the lisper sweet his rattle,
Nor for the other the piano ring;
But I can aid my boy-child in his prattle,
And I can prompt my girl-child how to sing.

"I cannot lead them to the daisied meadows,
But I can over-look them when they're there;
And give a golden glow to passing shadows,
And make the fair sunshine to them more fair.

"I cannot give them supper in the even,
Nor on the morn to them their toast convey;
But when they kneel before the Lord of heaven,
Them I can prompt for what and how to pray.

" Ay, tho' they cannot see or hear me, ever
    Into the soul of babe and father flows
The presence of their mourn'd one like a river,
    That wakens music where-so-e'er it goes.

"So, as by those the idols of my bosom,—
    Touch'd by the carol of the unseen bird ;
Touch'd by the perfume of the unseen blossom,
    The hearts of others to their depths are stirr'd.

"Nay, by each spirit sweet with whom my spirit
    In state harmonic moved and breathed, I'm felt ;
And still alive to every form of merit,
    Still dwells my love with those with whom it dwelt.

"Alive to these—to each high aspiration—
    To every base-born passion yet alive ;
To all that tendeth to man's elevation,—
    To all that downward doth the spirit drive.

"Alive to all most worthy to be cherish'd,
    Alive to all should most excite our dread :
And being thus, albeit the body's perish'd,
    How can it be averr'd that I am dead ?"

ROBIN REDBREAST.

'Tis little Robin Redbreast
    Was piping on the spray,
"And pray, mamma, what shall we do
    To bring him up this way?"
Mamma into the pantry goes,
    And out again she comes,
And up flies the piper sweet,
    To pick up the crumbs.

I laughed to see the birdie pick,
    And clapt my hands in mirth,
When pussy up her ears did prick,
    Was lying on the hearth:
The nasty puss from out the house,
    Now at the piper springs;
But off unhurt darts Robin
    Upon his little wings.

"You cruel Tab, what would you do?—
    Mamma, reach me the cane,
And I will teach her Queenship how
    To play such pranks again:"
Around the room I pussy ran,
    And vainly ran her long,
The while away upon the spray
    Sweet Robin piped his song.

ARACHNE.

I READ in an old book the myth
Of the Hellenian damsel with
The magic needle, when there fell
On me a power—a mystic spell—
I could not well to others tell,
But all at once my soul was swept
Into a sphere where sorrow kept
Her vigils sad. There on my ear
Awoke in accents deep, yet clear:

"The guerdon of my heavy sin
Forever thus I toil and spin
The fatal cord, the lash accursed,
By which my heavy woe is nursed."

"From whence this wail?" I inly asked,
When thro' the gloom I saw unmasked
One, from whose thin wan face and look,
I for the needle-worker took;
And lifting up my voice I said :—
"And art thou she of whom I've read—
Arachne's self?" No answer made
The image pale, nor turned, nor fled
Nor into air, thin air dissolved:
But while within my thoughts revolved,

A something on my vision loom'd,
Tho' what it was might be presumed
Not clearly seen, at least by one
Still bound to earth by flesh and bone;
But whatsoe'er it was or meant,
Anon thereon her gaze was bent,
And this way that, her white hands went,
Whilst to their motion keeping time,
Re-woke upon my ear the chime:

"The guerdon of my ebon sin,
Forever thus I toil and spin,
The fatal cord, the lash accursed,
By which my heavy woe is nursed.

" The sun and moon, they come and go,
The ocean's waters ebb and flow;
My baleful star must even burn,
My swollen tide know no return.

" Woe, woe the day, woe, woe the day
I first did feel that piercing ray,
Beneath whose magic touch, behold,
The rock's converted into gold.

" Ah, from that hour did earth become
To me a glad, a jewell'd home;
Where-e'er I turned enrapt I viewed,
A living fact the fair and good.

"Where-e'er I turned enrapt I viewed,
A living fact the fair and good,
Which to my spirit's chambers sped,
And with the inner beauty wed.

"As casquets in which gems are shrined,
So from the lustre of my mind,
My body borrowed splendour, till
My presence stood a living will.

"Entranced I took the web and wrought
A vision so with beauty fraught,
The gazer held his breath and crept
Into himself, and smiled and wept.

"Delusive tears, delusive smiles,
What were you but the serpent's toils?—
The nectar sparkling in yon cup,
To writhe the lips that quaff it up?

"Flushed with success, I then did cast
A scornful glance upon the past,
And from that moment I began
A course which ended in this ban.

"The very God within me burns;
My soul a mortal triumph spurns;
Not mortals, o'er immortals must
I stride, or perish in the dust.

"Thus frantically cried I, when
Was flashed upon my inner ken
Minerva's might and sheen, and I,—
What was there left me but to die?

"A meteor in the night, her might,
And sheen is flashed upon my sight;
But as the night by meteor cleft,
My soul again in gloom is left,

"I view the den in which I crawl,
I view what doth my soul appal;
But ah, ere I my plight can mend,
All hope to me hath found an end.

"And now instead of sylvan ground,
Where grief was lost, where joy was found;
My path is such each step I take,
Awakes the hissing of the snake.

"My night is still by horrors throng'd,
My day is but that night prolong'd;
The sun may set, the sun may rise,
No soothing slumber seals my eyes.

"Around, beneath, and over-head,
The finger of the Living Dread
Has fix'd a curse which see—What's this
Would thus o'er-brim my heart with bliss?

" Yes, yes my hand that vision traced,
Mine ivory brow with wreaths are graced ;
Aloud my pean's sung, aloud,
And she my rival's head down bowed.

" No, never since the world begun,
Was ever such a triumph won
By mortal or immortal—sped
My dream ? or dream I now instead ?

"The sun and moon they come and go,
The ocean's waters ebb and flow,
My baleful star must ever burn,
My swollen tide know no return.

" And, such the guerdon of my sin
Thus, thus to toil, and thus to spin
The fatal cord, the lash accursed,
By which my heavy woe is nursed."

Thus mourned the damsel ; while she mourn'd
Back into sense my soul return'd ;
At which receded from my sight
The needle-worker's image. Light
Was breaking in the orient, yet,
Not till again the sun had set,
Could I forget her wail—nor then,
Nay, even till this hour, the strain —

"The guerdon of my heavy sin
Forever this I toil and spin,"
Will break upon my inner ear,
And down my cheek will steal a tear,
For one whom Fame in days of old
Crowned with her brightest wreath, and bold,
And brave, and wise, alike proclaimed
The glory of that gift which framed
What their own triumphs shamed.

THE THEFT.

PERFIDIOUS damsel, with thy dazzling eyes,
Those skill'd enchanters of a sunnier clime,
Thou, thou hast charmed the dragon Reason, couched
Before my soul's Hesperides, and filched
Her fruit of burnished ore—the source itself
From which her splendour sprung—her will, and left—
Yea, naked left her to the winds of woe :
And now, while she laments her jewels lost,
With scorn dost hie to mock, to drive afar,
The veriest promise of a summer, would
Again enable her to smile, and with
Her golden apples set the world agape.

LOST AT THE FAIR.

Last night at the Fair did I lose thee, my honey—
I hunted thee south and I hunted thee north ;
I'd rather than lost thee have lost all the money
That all the great lords in the kingdom are worth.

Chorus.—Heart-sorry in worry in flurry did hurry
      Poor I, like a wild thing alost, here and there,
      When Rosy the cosy, sweet Rosy the posy
      And pride of her Robin, was miss'd at the Fair.

Resolved to discover the fleet-footed rover,
  My way thro' the stalls, shows, and people I wound ;
But there 'mid ways many, the rarest of any,
  No image like Rose's sweet image was found.

    Chorus.—Heart-sorry in worry and flurry, etc.

With glee the Inns sounded, with joyance unbounded
  Danced maiden and callant ; I into them glanced ;
But who was who barely I saw, tho' saw fairly
  That no one like Rose with the dancers a-danced.

    Chorus.—Heart-sorry in worry and flurry, etc.

In search of my honey I spent all my money,
Then took to the road in a spirit of gloom,
When lo, with my Rosy I met, and the posy
I kiss'd her and cuddled her all the way home.

Chorus.—Heart-sorry in worry in flurry did hurry
Poor I, like a wild thing alost, here and there;
Till lo, with my Rosy I met, and the posy
I kiss'd, sung, and linked with her home from the Fair.

"GET UP!"

"Get up!" the caller calls, "Get up!"
 And in the dead of night,
To win the bairns their bite and sup,
 I rise a weary wight.

My flannel dudden donn'd, thrice o'er
 My birds are kiss'd, and then
I with a whistle shut the door
 I may not ope again.

THE BRIDAL GIFT.

LAST night at the fair I met light-footed Polly,
   And Nanny from Earsdon and bothersome Nell,
And yellow-hair'd Bessy and hazel-eyed Dolly;
   But Rosy for sweetness did bear off the bell.

Chorus.—Not Polly, nor Dolly, nor coy little Bell;
        Not Nanny nor Fanny, nor sly little Nell;
        Not Bessy, nor Jessy, is loved half so well
          As Rosy the posy—la, no!

A bridal gift to her—a rich snowy feather,
   To put in her bonnet—a locket I bought;
A hand-bag beside of the best foreign leather;
   A pair of fine gloves and with figures enwrought.

      Chorus.—Not Polly, nor Dolly, etc.

A silken scarf gave I with silver lace laced, and
   A rarely cut comb for her tresses so dear;
A rich broider'd girdle to girdle her waist, and
   A Guinea gold droplet to hang at each ear.

      Chorus.—Not Polly, nor Dolly, etc.

A bonny bit brooch did I buy for her bosom ;
A mantle of scarlet, a bonny white gown ;
The garland I'd promised of sweet orange blossom,
The ring that shall make her forever my own.

Chorus.—Not Polly, nor Dolly, etc.

Some gifts to my honey I bought, and had money
Been mine I to these had link'd castles and lands,
And Nan, Nell, and Polly, and Fan, Bell, and Dolly,
Had danced in her train and obeyed her commands.

Chorus.—Not Polly, nor Dolly, nor coy little Bell ;
Not Nanny nor Fanny, nor sly little Nell ;
Not Bessy, nor Jessy, is loved half so well
As Rosy the posy—la, no !

THE MYSTIC LYRE.

HEAVEN-GIFTED was the mortal, thrice-illum'ed by heaven's
    own fire,
A bard the chords of whose great soul to love and truth
    were strung,   [lyre
Who deemed the mighty universe itself a seven-stringed
From which at the Creator's touch the anthem, Life, is
    wrung.

An instrument it is by which a gamut vast is spann'd,
    Whose every tone's in unison with every other tone;
And which alone is given to the heart to understand
    Who to pity gives an ear of soul—to self an ear of stone.

To such a one the accents of that magic lyre expound
    The kinship of all beings great and small, and how the
        sweet
Yet mighty octave to the key struck in yon planet's found
    Within the little dew-drop that sparkles at our feet.

In the seeming great the little, in the seeming small the
    great,
Are rendered by that music to the pure in spirit, plain;
And the thistle's and the lily's and the mourn'd and envied
    state
Are but altos and contraltos in one bright harmonic
    strain.

In the seeming ill the good is, in the seeming good the ill;
  But in Life's complex measure what the ill deplored appears,
Is often but a needful step into a varied trill [and fears.
  That terminates with rapture what began mid doubts

All height and depth of moral being are compass'd in one chant,
  And thro' vast scales descending in the lowest soul is heard
True echoes, true, tho' faint, of what the highest soul can vaunt,
  Whilst to the lowest full as oft the highest yields a chord.

The measure of the man with all his destiny so vast,
  When the key-note of the living known is stricken may be shown;
And the burden of the future and the burden of the past,
  Are but coloured octaves to the note from out the present thrown.

The measure of the angel in the measure of the man,
  Yea, he the highest seraph in the lowest serf's concealed;
And the diapason struck on earth compriseth in its span,
  An echo of the heaven itself in angel-states reveal'd.

Not that which was, is that which is, as sang the Hebrew sage, [turn,
  But a duller to a brighter chord; and that which is, in
Is but a stage in life's great march prophetic of a stage
  That awaits the soul's arrival when we leap death's dreaded bourn.

The mighty universe itself is but a mighty lyre,
  From which at the Creator's touch the anthem, Life, is flung;
And could we heed its music, up would leap our souls on fire,
  And up a hymn to Love Eterne would leap from every tongue!

THE DEWDROP.

Ah, be not vain. In yon flower-bell,
  As rare a pearl, did I appear,
As ever grew in ocean shell,
  To dangle at a Helen's ear.

So was I till a cruel blast
  Arose and swept me to the ground,
When, in the jewel of the past,
  Earth but a drop of water found.

AWAY TO THE FAIR.

(The chorus is old.)

Away to the Fair, my lad did repair
  Ere day had the welkin adorned;
Now day's glidden by and night's in the sky,
  And he, he has never returned:
Now day's glidden by, coal-black is the sky,
  And, tho' a dead calm's in the air,
O'er mountain and plain, a storm brews amain—
  And Willie comes not from the Fair.

Chorus—O dear, what can the matter be?
  O dear, what can the matter be?
  Dear, dear, what can the matter be
  Willie comes not from the Fair?

Came Tam cap a-gley with Robin, and he
  But nodded to Bell o'er the way;
And Robin did call on Tib at the Hall,
  But naught of his neighbour did say:
And Allie went by, a laugh in his eye
  For Meg of the Collirce Square;
But never a word of Willie was heard—
  And Willie comes not from the Fair.

Chorus—O, dear, etc.

AWAY TO THE FAIR. 115

I ended my wark while lilted the lark
   "Tere-lere" to his grass-hidden mate;
And drest in my best, a rose in my breast,
   I've waited his coming—and wait:
The door set ajar, the fire I stir,
   And, often a-combing my hair,
I hark for the beat of two merry feet—
   But Willie comes not from the Fair.

   Chorus—O dear, etc.

"What ails the jewel?" my mother, she cries;
   "Ye're white as the cap on your head;"
"An imp's in the lass," my father replies;
   "Let, let her be off to her bed."
Atween hearth and door, I wander the floor,
   A-deaf to their bidding and prayer;
And halt but to keek in the storm-rock'd night—
   But Willie comes not from the Fair.

   Chorus—O dear, etc.

Now fear fills the house—some shriek from affright:
   The dog howls aloud by the hearth;
For runnels of fire do flash thro' the night,
   And deep thunder growls shake the earth:
On high, at each growl, "Tu-whit," cries the owl;
   "Tu-whoo!" while the windows declare,
In terrific screams, how the fierce rain teems—
   And Willie's not come from the Fair.

   Chorus—O dear, etc.

AWAY TO THE FAIR.

Away dies the storm, and up peers the moon
    To brighten a cloud black as death;
While a clear cock-crow succeeds to the tune,
    The storm piped the while he had breath:
Now sleeps the whole house—save cricket and mouse,
    I oft to the window repair,
And start at each sound: but the hours go round—
    And Willie comes not from the Fair.

    Chorus—O dear, etc.

The night weareth old, to bed I must go,
    But neither to slumber nor rest;
The thought of my lad the weary night, so
    Will pierce like a thorn in my breast:
But up with the lark, to granny's I'll down,
    For if he's arrived he'll be there;
And if he is not, I'll off to the town
    And seek for him all thro' the Fair.

Chorus—O dear, what can the matter be?
    O dear, what can the matter be?
    Dear, dear, what can the matter be
    Willie comes not from the Fair?

MUSIC.

I LISTEN to the accents of the silver corded harp
And tho' aweary of the darts at me by malice hurl'd
Aflying goes life's shuttle and aflying woof and warp—
A renovated soul I seek to renovate the world.

As spring is to the brooklet bound in winter's icy chain,
  As showers are to the blossoms parch'd by summer's hottest breath;
As sleep is to the body bow'd by toil and rack'd by pain,
  So is music to this heart to whom the jars of life are death.

The bonds in which I'm bound are broken by its magic power, [that please;
And pent up founts of feeling flow in looks and acts
And refreshened as the lily is refreshened by the shower,
  The soul from trouble freed in turn the frame from trouble frees.

Nay, not freed alone from trouble, not alone by pleasure fill'd— [restored;
Not alone to strength of body and to peace of mind
I'm thrill'd and by a feeling that the ancients may have thrill'd
  When they sang the golden truths and taught what later times ignored.

Taught by the glamour under which I labour, bright and
    clear
  Become to me the darkest legends of an elder day;
And so-called myths thus said or sung by bards illumined,
    wear
  The colours which the True itself and not the False array.

'Tis said that to the Amphionic song, sun-like, up-rose
  The Hundred-Gated City, and howe'er this be I know
At music's touch a tower-girt citadel my spirit glows,
  Thro' whose illumined corridors no hydra-doubt may go.

Not mine to under-go what under-went Arion, yet,
  From out a darker sea, the waters of affliction caught,
And on a brighter than a Tenarian shore I'm set
  To marvel at the miracle a melody has wrought.

Not mine Orpheus-like the gift to strike the lyre and chant
  What from another Pluto had another captive charmed;
But mine to know a lesser gift has made despair to grant
  What Pluto's gruesome regions had a place of pleasure
    form'd.

Nay, not a feeler merely, but an actor keen am I,
  Empower'd to seize the harp of life and from its cords
    to bring
An anthem such as had compelled Apollo's self to sigh,
  And wrung from him the palm Marsyas tried in vain
    to wring.

Away into the regions of delight and, what is more,
　　Away into the regions of the inner life I'm borne
To learn how Nature at one birth both light and music bore,
　　And how the planets danced and sung upon Creation's morn.

At this the giddy world may laugh; their jibes are spent in vain;—
　　I stand above and far above the arrows at me flung:—
So chant I music fired—and whatever worth my strain,
　　For men of brain, not stocks and stones, and men of soul 'tis sung.

THE BUTTERFLY.

The butterfly from flower to flower
　　The urchin chased; and, when at last,
He caught it in my lady's bower,
　　He cried, "Ha, ha!" and held it fast.

Awhile he laugh'd, but soon he wept,
　　When looking at the prize he'd caught
He found he had to ruin swept
　　The very glory he had sought.

SLIGHTED.

Ah me! my heart is like to break,
The envied rose upon my cheek,
The blood red rose is cold and bleak
    Now Robin slighteth me.

Alas! a shadow lone and pale
I all unheard my lot bewail;
He listens to another's tale,
    He hath no ear for me.

Could he but look upon my grief
Would he not try to bring relief?
I feel my days below are brief,
    So deep the wound I dree.

I trail about I know not how;
I like a thief slink down the row,
For well behind my back I know
    The rest all laugh at me.

The rest to one the other wink
Whenever down the row I slink;
Their hearts are filled with glee to think
    How he my bane should be.

SLIGHTED. 121

The very bairns have caught their words,
As notes are caught by mocking birds,
By jibes are rent my bosom chords,
    And grief is killing me.

I feel my days on earth are brief;
Ah! could he look upon my grief
Would he not try to bring relief?
    Would he not kinder be?

I dreamed last night to me he came;
A blush was on his cheek for shame;
He took my hand, he breathed my name;
    He gave such looks to me—

Such looks? No sun will rise to set
When I forget those looks, forget
Those star-bright eyes, those eyes of jet
    That wiled my heart from me.

The vision fled, and I was left
To mourn a lot of hope bereft—
To mourn what won my heart, and cleft,
    And oh, the agony!

Dear Robin—Dear? Without a peer,
And yet to me so dear, so dear!
Ah, fare-thee-well! and may'st thou ne'er
    Be doomed to sigh like me!

THE MODEST MAID.

O, COULD I a garland braid,
That would never, never fade,
I would crown the modest maid
    Queen of earth's joy-giving band!
Poor or wealthy, dark or fair,
Lo, that happy one's an heir
To a dowery as rare
    As e'er fell from fortune's hand!

Not the look which once to spy,
Would the stoic's pride destroy,
Could to my astonished eye,
    Her endearing looks eclipse;
Not the music which to hear,
Would dispel the cynic's sneer,
Could to my astonished ear
    Spoil the music of her lips!

Let the haughty beauty frown;
Let the wretch her rigour own;
Once her mid-day splendour flown,
    Banished is her boasted power:
Whereas she that's modest wears
Dearer with the march of years;
Yea, like yonder sun appears
    Grandest in her setting hour!

THE OUTCAST FLOWER.

You turn up your nose at me ? I suppose,
 I'm noisome and base ?
Before on my head you cruelly tread,
 Give ear to my case.

A lily-bell rare, my charms were laid bare,
 And lo ! at the sight,
In a mantle of gold, a delight to behold,
 Love danced in delight.

To him I was dear—ah me ! it was clear
 That nothing above,
Below, or around, by Love could be found,
 So precious to love.

That little white flower which gildeth the hour
 When March winds rave,
The snowdrop, as clear from stain might appear,
 But look'd too grave.

The crocus a-drest in her sun-given vest,
 On Spring's live mould,
To her heart's delight, might sparkle as bright,
 But look'd too bold.

THE OUTCAST FLOWER.

No zephyr did woo a hyacinth blue,
    With bearing so fine;
No daffodil e'er did view in the mere
    A face so divine.

The tulip so gay a cheek might display
    In deeper hues dyed;
But where the sweet smell?—could any one tell?—
    The dancer enjoyed?

The pink had a bloom as rich in perfume,
    To make the heart glad;
But where was the grace to rivet the gaze
    The lily-bell had?

Not even the rose, the richest that blows,
    Could Love then prefer;
And the pansy, so sweet, bowed down at her feet,
    In homage to her.

This swore Love, and, sworn, away I was torn,
    His pleasure to be;
But ere a day past away I was cast—
    He cared not for me.

Unheeded I pined, my sweets did the wind
    No longer perfume;
To vile turned the pure—the sweet turned a sour—
    Ah, such was my doom.

You turn up your nose ! just think of my woes,
    Though base to behold,
Just think ere you tread—ere you crush my poor head—
    Just think what I've told.

THE MOTH.

To-night a gilded moth took wing,
    And round-a-round yon wax-light flew;
And, while his flight did her enring,
    He nearer to the dazzler drew.

"So fair art thou," he cried, "to view,
    I'd die upon thy lips to feed;"
And so must snatch a kiss and rue—
    Ah, he was murder'd for the deed.

THE TOAST.

I'M as loyal a subject as Britain can boast;
   Our Queen she is gracious, and gentle, and wise;
But another this moment demandeth my toast,—
   'Tis Annie, the lass with the two hazel eyes.

The hair of my idol's a stream of delight,
   The lustre thereof with the aerolite vies;
Her dimpled cheeks apples, the pure red and white;
   But these are outshone by her two hazel eyes.

Her breasts are two hillocks of new-driven snow,
   Between them a dell of enchantment lies,
Where love lurks, the elf! with his death-darts, but no—
   These cannot be named with her two hazel eyes.

The golden-eyed lily but faintly displays
   The grace of her form, her demeanour, and guise;
A jewel is she in heart, language, and ways;
   But nothing can equal her two hazel eyes.

I'm as loyal a subject as Britain can boast;
   Victoria's gentle, gracious, and wise;
But another this moment demanded my toast,—
   I drink to the lass with the two hazel eyes.

TWO HAZEL EYES.

WAS ever a bard in such pitiful plight?
Was ever such seen by yon stars in the skies?
A-pit or a-bed—by day and by night,
I'm plagued by the magic of two hazel eyes.

A leaf in a whirlwind, I'm sent to and fro,
And peace, panic-stricken, my bosom still flies;
For rest I implore, but my portion below
Is the rest-killing magic of two hazel eyes.

The world it goes up, and the world it goes down,
And the lofty descend, and the lowly arise;
But fortune, the jilter, may smile or may frown,
I feel but the magic of two hazel eyes.

Once blithe as a linnet I lilted my lay,
And won the applause of both foolish and wise—
Now deaf, dumb, derided, I go on my way,
Bewitched by the magic of two hazel eyes.

O Annie, wouldst thou but look down on my plight,
And pity my case, and no longer despise,
I'd dance in delight, I'd sing day and night,
And the theme of my lays be thy two hazel eyes!

OMEGA.

WRAPT in fancy by a river,
That flows onward ever, ever,
Down I sat me while the moon
In her fairest vesture shone—
All was still as death, when lo!
Down the solemn tide did flow
Fays that once with pleasure thrill'd me,—
Fiends that once with horror chill'd me—
Social Glee and sullen Care,
Lofty Courage, crouching Fear,
And—ah! who with dire Despair?
She on whom my heart has hung,
She who oft my heart has strung,
While the heavy-footed years,
Sought to bury her in cares!
"One by one, and two by two,
They the graceful, they the true,
Went my idols long ago,
And must thou desert me now?"
 Thus I frantically cried,
When a look was cast behind,
Clung—shall cling unto my mind,
 And a hollow voice replied;—
"All things go the way we're going,
 From thy quest refrain—
All, all that be—the Earth, the Sea,

OMEGA.

Yon Moon above, the Stars that move
In concord o'er yon crystal plain;
Yea, all to one vast gulph are flowing,
And thy cry's in vain?"

Heard I aright, what is my cry
A cry in vain? what means reply
So dark as this? Can earth and sky—
Can all my hope, my pride, my joy,
With earth and sky take wing and fly?

Can that for which I've daily borne
With insult, empty scoff and scorn,
For which I've labour'd still to earn,
'Till Life itself's a burden grown—
Can that one day from me be flown?

Can that for which I've inly bled,
And tears of blood, not water shed;
For which I've lain on thorny bed,
Who else had lain on bed of down—
Can that one day from me be flown?

Can that for which I've wooed disgrace—
Look'd Persecution in the face;
For which I've barter'd pelf and place,
And donn'd instead the martyr's crown—
Can that one day from me be flown?

What can the all my soul hold dear,
The soul itself and all whate'er
　Comprised in this Great Universe
Take wing and never more return?
　Can Life itself thus prove a curse,
And mock the mighty souls who yearn
Even to obtain the life superne—
　Sung in prophetic verse?

Forbid it Truth!—" It is forbid!"
Rang in my soul as voice ne'er did,
A voice whose tone the quester chid;—
" It is forbid. On facts alone
From battle with externals won,
The common understanding may
Persist another thing to say;
But whoso looks Life's surface under
The Veil of Isis seeks to sunder,
And on internals cares to ponder,
Even such a one will find whate'er
Has been will be, tho' Earth's rude sphere
To outer sense should disappear—
Tho' to that sense, above, below,
All things appear to come and go,
Yet to the inner living still
With dread to chill, with bliss to thrill -
To warn, encourage, pain or charm,
To lead to blessedness, or harm;
To whip or bless us for the act
Another's heart has soothed or racked;
Yea, all things and all deeds whatever
　Shall to the inner sense remain —

Shall constitute a fountain ever
Of what should nerve for high endeavour—
Of what, once drank, should heart and brain,
So fire that Man, would rue ah, never!
    That he was born tho' born to pain—
    Thy cry is not in vain."

THE ORACLE.

The vision will vanish for ever,
    That gildeth this moment thy track ;
And in vain were the noblest endeavour
    To call the enchantment back.

Yet pine not; a balm—an ovation
    Is thine in the thought, that the day
Will come when thy bleak desolation
    Will pass like thy vision away.

ALL IS VANITY.

From all that I have seen or heard
    This world, is but an empty show,
And only can the heart afford
    What tends to bitter strife and woe;
Nay in its clutch, do what we will,
    Upon our erring steps attend
Annoyance and vexation still,
    To cross and wrack us to the end.

That bubble frail, in sheen unmatched,
    Attracted by its radiance rare,
Do we stretch out our hand to snatch't?
    The jewel melts into the air:
So will the golden wish we prize
    Seem all but in our fingers locked,
And then evanish from our eyes,
    And leave us tantalized and mocked.

Does glory captivate the soul?
    Do we for bay or laurel crave?
And do we seek the distant goal
    Assured the prize is for the brave?

ALL IS VANITY.

Years roll away and life is past
  And in the end what at the most,
For sleepless nights and labours vast,
  What have we but a blank to boast?

To drink we fly in woe, and drunk
  Is thus what makes us fools—in fact
Down to a lower level sunk,—
  The brute, in brutal acts, to act;
Again becoming self-possess'd,
  What rankles in his bosom—ay
What but a ten times direr pest
  Than that from which we strove to fly?

By beauty's dazzling spells beset,
  The strong, the weak, the grave, the gay,
On locks of gold, on eyes of jet,
  May dream the transient hours away;
May dream to wake, and what? to learn
  Those locks are worse than serpents fell;
Those eyes but fires of hate and scorn,
  Ordained to make our life a hell.

The supple knee we yield to gold,
  And seek for happiness in pelf;
And what's our gain but cares untold?
  And what's our loss but manhood's self?
We lose what gold has never bought,
  We gain but what degrades the man,
And for the happiness thus sought
  We yet may find it—when we can.

Deluded still are we! and should
 We grasp at last the boon esteemed,
The victim of a ban then would
 We deem it other than we deemed;
Then let thy vain endeavour end,
 Its promised blessings let them go,
Unto thy spirit's weal attend —
 This world is but an empty show!"

THE PARTIES.

Now Gladstone's party bears the bell,
 And now Disraeli's—now
The people really cannot tell,
 For whom their hands to show.

Now this way, la, now that inclined,
 A giddy vane they go,
The victim of each puff of wind
 The party bugles blow.

1868.

THE SOCIAL GLASS.

Air—"Rosson the Beau."

Come fill up the glass, and tho' never
    We tasted of gladness before,
The thought of this moment for ever
    Shall gladden the heart to its core :
An isle as we sail o'er life's ocean—
    An isle shall this moment remain,
On which we'll look back with emotion,
    And long to salute it again !

    Chorus—Come fill up the glass, etc.

Let the miser exult in his treasure ;
    The king in his sceptre and crown ;
The lover be loved without measure ;
    The warrior blest with renown ;
We envied no mortal his blisses,
    When anguish our bosom hath torn ;
And tasting such treasure as this is,
    We laugh every other to scorn.

    Chorus—Come fill up the glass, etc.

Since the life-giving goblet is given,
    Man may be oppressed by the day,
But the links of oppression are riven
    When night brings its spell into play :
That spell so excelling's united
    All other fair spells in its train,
To enjoy which, ho ! ho ! you're invited
    To pass round the goblet again.

    Chorus—Come fill up the glass, etc.

A WORD OF GOOD CHEER.

Why thus mourn o'er star-hopes faded?
　They are only from thy ken,
By a passing vapour shaded,
　And will soon appear again :
Up and guard thee like a warrior,
　Up and make the present thine ;
Trust me every doubt's a barrier
　To Life's heritage divine.

See, yon kingly soul attended
　By the dulcet tones of love—
An immortal here descended
　But to lift our eyes above ;
Dark as be thy lot and cruel,
　He has known as dire a woe ;
Bright as be his prize, a jewel
　Brighter still for thee may glow.

Not the Cytherean—truly
　Vain its pursuit and unwise,
But the joy Uranian, duly
　Seek we that, and rich the prize ;

A WORD OF GOOD CHEER.

But for that be our endeavour,
   And afar our doubt and fear,
We shall then be losers never,
   Tho' but losers we appear.

Lose we may the husk and perish
   What the outer senses prize,
But no real joy we cherish
   Ever from us fades or flies;
Hid it may be from the spirit,
   Only for awhile 'tis hid,
And one day will meed our merit,
   With a joy to sense forbid.

From our bosom the infernal—
   All that's mean, and low, and base,
Every wish and longing carnal
   Chase we then, or seek to chase;
Clearer to us then and clearer
   Would Life's complex riddle seem,
And our Edens fled prove nearer,
   Than at present we may deem.

He the lord of his own passions,
   Peers the monarch ne'er so bold—
For his loins a girdle fashions
   Richer than a girth of gold:

Not a thorn can pierce his bosom
  But—before the pang has flown—
But becometh a bright blossom
  His right royal head to crown.

"Valour's born from self-denial,
  Wisdom from each stern rebuke,
Power from every pain and trial
  That the human soul may brook;"
Sagest heroes, heroic sages,
  So have taught since Time began;
Up, then, earn a hero's wages,
  Up, then up, and be a man.

Up! and lo! to hail thee victor
  Smiles will leap from every brook;
Beauty will herself impicture
  On whatever thou mayst look.
Stars—the blessed stars, my brother,
  Will attend thee in the night;
And Creation's self be other
  Than it seems to common sight.

MY LITTLE BOY.

My little boy, thy laughter
   Goes to my bosom core,
And sends me yearning after
   The days that are no more

Adown my cheek is stealing
   A briny tear, and I—
But let no selfish feeling
   Thy infant mirth destroy.

Fill not with looks so earnest,
   Those pretty eyes of thine;
A lot were thine the sternest,
   Couldst thou my thought divine.

There's time enough for sorrow,
   When Life's pale eve draws near;
The lark lilts thee Good Morrow:
   Ring out thy laughter clear!

THE STAINED LILY.

When first the maiden fair I eyed,
   —This world is a world of grief alone—
A lily she held and a rose beside—
   But I was doomed her lot to moan.

The rose was gain'd and the lily was stain'd,
   —This world is a world of grief alone—
And from that hour her beauty waned,
   And I was left her lot to moan.

The lily was stain'd when the rose was gain'd,
   —This world is a world of grief alone—
And from that hour her life star waned,
   And I was left her lot to moan.

Ah, never more in my sight she'll stand
   —This world is a world of grief alone—
With a lily bright in her lily-white hand,
   And I am doomed her lot to moan.

THE VIOLET AND THE ROSE.

The Violet invited my kiss,—
 I kiss'd it and called it my bride;
"Was ever one slighted like this?"
 Sighed the Rose as it stood by my side.

My heart ever open to grief,
 To comfort the fair one I turned;
"Of fickle ones thou art the chief!"
 Frown'd the Violet, and pouted and mourned

Then to end all disputes, I entwined
 The love-striken blossoms in one;
But that instant their beauty declined,
 And I wept for the deed I had done!

THE RESOLVE.

In trumpet-toned accents I heard
   A voice in a vision to cry;—
"By threat of no tyrant deterred,
   We rear up our banner on high.

"No longer, tho' feeble and poor,
   We'll wear out our days in the dust,
Our freedom we're sworn to procure,
   And have it or perish we must.

"Far better we rush to the grave,
   The bed of each mortal at last,
Than eat the vile bread of the slave—
   Than pine as we've pined in the past.

"The life of the hero's a boon,
   A blossom the meanest must prize;
The life of the faint-hearted loon,
   A weed that the noble despise.

"Then up," cried the voice, and I thought,
   While loud the deep accents yet rang,
A turbann'd oppressor was brought,
   To think of his deeds with a pang.

1878.

GOD AND THE RIGHT.

(1878.)

Let England beware ere war she declare,
   She earn not the mark of the beast
By marching her power the State to secure
   Of blood-imbued wolf of the East ;
The Bulgarian, he, and Servian dree
   Such wrongs, from their foeman, as might
Cause stones, could they speak, to cry " for the weak
   Be thou—and for God and the Right ! "

Such horrific crimes belong to past times ;
   The coldest and hardest heart bleeds—
A blush for our race be-crimsons each face,
   When named are the Turk and his deeds ;
Too awful are they to utter, nor may
   Men know them and know a respite
From heart-ache till they have armed for the fray,
   And battle for God and the Right !

An unbounded thirst for lucre accurst,
   The helpless must sate—even so—
In this should they fail they're fated to wail
   The blood-bringing lash of the foe ;
In glee will the Turk his victim so work,
   Such anguish inflict, at the sight,
The veriest serf grasps his sabre, resolved
   To battle for God and the Right.

GOD AND THE RIGHT.

See! dearer than life, the daughter and wife,
    A prey to the torturer's lust;
The Rayah heart-torn, yet ridiculed, mourn
    His losses 'mid ashes and dust;
His dear home despoiled, his dear ones defiled,
    A wreck what was once his delight—
What wonder if he, in delirium, flee
    To battle for God and the Right:

The temple is burned, the altar's o'erturned,—
    With blood the street runnelets run;
The prey bird and beast hie swiftly to feast
    On corpses that rot in the sun;
The ban-dog's harsh tones, while crashing the bones,
    Are heard by the brave in the night;
But heard with a cry, death to hear, and they fly
    To battle for God and the Right:

For God and the Right the Rebel States fight;
    And whate'er the sequel—oh, oh:
If thou too must fight, for God and the Right,
    Fight thou, in the vanguard, fight thou:
The gold-kings may howl and threaten and scowl,
    Yet hold to thy purpose and smite,
Smite thou the proud Turk till he finds 'tis bad work
    To war against God and the Right.

THE BROOKLET.

A LITTLE brooklet trilled a song
As merry as the day was long,
At which a music-hater stung
To frenzy said : " I'll bind thy tongue,
And quell thy merriment : " That night,
A dam check'd babbler's song and flight ;
But blind are ever hate and spite !
And so it fell, the brook did swell—
Ah, truth to say, ere dawn of day,
Had grown a sea, unquelled would be,
And soon with ruin, down the dell,
Dashed with a fierce triumphant yell ;
And cried, " Ha, ha ! ho, ho ! oh, la !
Where now thy skill, my voice to still ?—
Ah, dost thou find that he who'd bind
The tongue e'en of a rillet, may
Be doomed to hear instead, one day,
What shall with terror seize, control,
And wring with agony his soul ?—
In very deed then, reck the rede ! "
Thus yell'd the flood and onward swept ;
And music-hater heard and wept :
And so weep all who'd try, or long,
To render dumb the child of song .

UNCLE BOB.

Old Uncle Bob lay on the settle,
   At eventide, while on the hob,
"Ree-tee-riti-too" sang the kettle,
   And charmed the dear heart of old Bob.

"Ree-tee-riti-too" on his ears, long
   The ear-chaining melody played,
Till back on his mind rushed the years, long,
   Entombed, and he more than half said :

'Twas just such an even as this is,
   When down by the oak in the dell,
The bliss was made mine of all blisses,
   In glances I won from my Nell.

An August sun hung in the heaven,
   Or slowly went down o'er the hill,
When lilting her song to the even,
   The darling skipt over the rill.

From moss'd stone to moss'd stone she skipt, and
   Then up like a roe the hillside,
Anon pass'd the willow-tree tript, and
   Then, then what had Ellen espied ?

Had sight of my face the maid flurried?
  "Not flurried," I murmur'd—"Nay, nay!"
As plucking a harebell she hurried
  Again with her prize up the way.

The harebell consigned to her bosom,
  Her eyes seem'd to rivet; she viewed,
And still with a smile viewed the blossom,
  Till near to the spot where I stood;

Then raising her head and a golden
  Lock twisting, a word left her tongue,
Recall'd to my fancy an olden
  Time dearer than bard ever sung.

That time now of times—ah, an olden
  Time dearer than bard ever sung;
And oh, for the glamour so golden,
  The moment that word left her tongue.

" Dear Robin," she said, and so sweetly
  She linked the word " dear " with my name,
My senses forsook me completely,
  And fierce delight shook my whole frame.

" Dear Nelly," said I, and the sweetest
  Of hands in my hands I then prest;
And the hour that ensued was the fleetest,
  That ever a mortal man blest.

Nay, while yet the words she had spoken
    Like silver bells rang in my ears,
I felt that a barrier was broken
    Had kept us asunder for years.

Then lived we the olden time over
    Again—ah, the sweetest of hours!
Ere years aid the mind to discover
    What cankers may lurk in life's flowers.

When at the eve-song of the ousel,
    Our hearts with a rapture would glow,
Would mock what his fiercest carousal
    Can on the mad Bacchant bestow.

Then, hand in hand skimmed we the meadow,
    Or up the deep valley would run
And find in the willow's cool shadow,
    A shield from the heat of the sun.

There sat we full often and prattled
    Of all we had done or would do,
And still from our little tongues rattled
    Whatever we fancied or knew.

Around its old stem oft we sported;
    And charmed with their colour or smell,
As oft 'neath its shade we assorted
    The blooms we had pluck'd in the dell.

That time of times dearest, that olden
    Time dearer than bard ever sung,
The meanest of flowers yet a golden
    Flower seem'd to this bosom when young.

The daisy we'd prize, coy and cosy,
    Its white cup, blood-rimm'd, and the gold
Of its eye made it worthy the posy
    Our mothers should smile to behold.

We'd there too the blue-bell which loveth
    To play with the breeze in the shade,
As eastward in spring-tide he moveth
    To heal the wounds winter hath made.

The cowslip was ours who with maiden
    Like modesty looks at the ground,
While winds with her riches are laden,
    And earth with her beauty is crown'd.

The woodbine we loved, and as truly
    The poppy that flared in the sun,
Whose cup black and crimson we duly
    Were taught by our mothers to shun.

To later born bloom as to early
    Our little hearts opened, or clung,
To darnel as primrose and rarely
    Oft while each we gathered, we sung.

And echo oft woke at our singing,
  Or laughed back our laughter aloud,
While down thro' the clear air came ringing
  A trill from the lark in the cloud.

That time of times dearest, that olden
  Time dearer than bard ever sung!
Thus fleeted so radiant and golden
  The hours when this bosom was young.

Thus fleeted the spring and the summer;
  Thus richer hued autumn went pass'd;
And welcome awaited the comer,
  When winter came on with a blast.

Then oft we with puft cheeks have striven
  To mock—the wind's bugles—and mocked
While oaks in his anger were driven
  And houses like cradles were rock'd.

Then loved we to see the snow falling
  In large feathery flakes to the ground;
And oft in each other snow-balling,
  An hour of pure rapture was found.

Then loved we the skater to view as
  He flew here and there in a trice;
And up for a clap our hands flew as
  He wrote out his name on the ice.

Then, then, when the brisk day had ended
  Then, then for the night that came down;
The hour I to Nelly then wended :—
  The welcome my errand would crown :

The father would hand me a cracket;
  The mother would smoothen my hair;
The sister would rax down my jacket,
  Or with me some dainty would share.

Then while round the table would story
  On story the elder folk tell,
Wee Robin was left in his glory
  To prate in the nook with wee Nell.

And so pass'd the time—time—that olden
  Time dearer than bard ever sung!
Then oh, for the dreams bright and golden
  That nightly their spells o'er us flung.

That time of times dearest, that olden
  Time dearer than bard ever sung!
Of this so we talk'd till the golden
  Sun sank and the Moon o'er us hung.

Then look'd up a moment the maiden
  And gazed on the planet above,
And I saw in her eyes a soul laden
  And sparkling with rapture and love.

Then gushed from those wells of pure beauty
    Such spells had my heart been a stone,
I'd felt as I felt then my duty,
    My love, and my all were her own.

Then tho' fail'd my speech crabb'd and broken,
    To speak what I'd do for her sake,
More golden words never were spoken
    Than seem'd to her ear what I spake.

Then claspt I her tight to my bosom ;
    And, ere that great moment had pass'd,
I kist and was kist by the blossom
    And—oh—that first kiss was our last.

I kiss'd and was kiss'd—love controlled in,
    That moment my arms round her cast,
We kiss'd and our feelings so golden !
    But oh that first kiss was our last.

Beneath a dark alder a devil
    In man's shape had lurk'd, and that hour
A tale of black import and evil
    Had enter'd her fond father's door

And from that loved door I was chidden
    Till raving and dying she lay—
Then to her bed-side I was bidden,
    But what could I then do or say ?

She perish'd the victim of slander;
And I from that time was oft eyed,
Alone in the night-tide to wander,
And pace for long hours the burnside.

And this would I do till from sorrow
And manifold labour and prayer
My soul did an angel's strength borrow
To break the strong bonds of despair.

"Then peace, peace was mine." On the settle
Unc turned here and saw at the hob
A little Nell using the kettle,
And "Tea tea," she said, "Uncle Bob."

BUBBLE-BLOWING.

From the pipe-end off it glides,
　Many hued appearing;
What, if cynic harsh derides,
　Sets the boys a-staring.
In their eyes gleam its dyes,
　Glow with radiance rarer
Till they cry "how bright! Yon sky
　Hath no planet fairer!"
Nay, nought else can be so fair,
　Naught, sir, more entrancing;
Blow it here, blow it there—
　Keep the bubble dancing!

Sailing thro' the air it goes,
　While the urchins stretching
Out their chins, upon their toes
　Blow the thing bewitching:
So blows Dick, and "ha, ha!" cries,
　At the image gazing,
"What is this salutes mine eyes?
　Truly it's amazing——"
"Eh, thy picture," Sue rejoins;
　And a-nearer glancing;
"Mine, too, in the crystal shines—
　Keep the bubble dancing!"

BUBBLE-BLOWING.

Blow it well—Bill and Bell,
    Blow in turn, and Jerry :
And in turn each discern
    What yet makes them merry ;
Merry, very! Scurvy loot—
    Little villain, scurvy,
Shout and blow, blow and shout,
    Wits a topsy-turvy ;
Even so agog they go
    On their hobbies prancing—
Blow and shout, shout and blow,
    Keep the bubble dancing.

"Fiddle-faddle fum is that!
    Understand me clearly—
I detest a ditty flat,
    Shouting, blowing merely : "
"Hear me out ! " " Well ? " " While they blow
    Bursts the magic wonder,
Leaving little Dick and Co.
    On their ways to ponder ; "
"Tut, what then ? " No look oblique—
    Then they seek, and chancing
To find other bubbles, seek,
    Seek to keep them dancing.

THE VISION.

I saw but once that lovely one,
  Nor need I see her twice to love ;
She broke upon me like the dawn,
  And o'er my soul her magic wove —
Yea, forced the lion stern to own
  Himself the captive of the dove.

She brought the morn, she left the night ;
  Nor strove I to throw off the chain ;
But rather felt a sweet delight
  To intermingle with the pain
That made my heart's repose a blight,
  Till madness ruled my thought's domain.

By night I sought a solitude,
  And gave unto the winds a grief
That struggled like the lava flood,
  That boils and struggles for relief ;
And night still left me in a mood
  Unto the voice of reason deaf.

The radiant planets in their flight,
  And she the quiet Queen of heaven,
With glory garmented the night ;
  But not to them the power was given
To kill, but rather nurse the blight
  By which afar my peace was driven.

Yet wished I not the sun to rise,
  For then the world were up, and then
Were I exposed to wistful eyes,
  And questions bold of forward men,
Who deem themselves both good and wise,
  Yet neither know nor pity pain.

And what on earth—ay, what in hell
  Can be more racking to the thought,
Than that our pangs unspeakable
  Should, disregarded, be as nought;
Or look'd upon with looks that tell
  In vain would sympathy be sought?

The magic vision fled, and so
  Have all those precious feelings, all!
Which gave to life a golden glow—
  Which made a joy this earthly ball—
And now, what's left to me? what, oh!
  What, but a cup of very gall?

I'M A-WEARY.

I'm a-weary with care, I'm a-weary with care,
Surrounded with woes that no mortal can bear;
Whil'st I gaze on the night of my ills and survey,
Not a star to direct my lorn soul on her way.

I'm shorn of my strength and the few are my years,
The winter of life on my aspect appears;
Ay, the feeling of death steals apace round my core,
Like the sea-waves around yon lone rock on the shore.

THE TWO VISIONS.

A GOLDEN sun went down to-night;
    When lo ! a vision from the olden
Time, flashed on my inner sight,
    With smiles more tender and as golden.

My blood ran cold; for I did know
    Another dream of equal splendour
Would follow that; but not with—O !
    Not with the golden smiles and tender.

THE SONGSTRESS.

The dearest accents ever heard
    Are thine my canny Sally—nay,
Thou art to me the sweetest bird
    That ever charmed the hours away.

I listen to each syllable
    Doth from thy lips of scarlet flow
And how I feel I cannot tell—
    But fain would feel forever so.

The stalest jest, the tritest tale,
    The rudest air, the longest song,
From thee were neither trite nor stale,
    From thee were neither rude nor long.

Thy music puts me in a trance,
    When I'm to heaviness inclined;
And maketh me in glee to dance,
    When I've no dancing in my mind.

The well-played lute, panpipe, or flute,
    May—must the tender heart enchant;
But neither flute, panpipe, or lute
    Had ever thy sweet tongue to vaunt.

SHE IS NOT FASHIONED.

She is not fashioned to command,
   Nor once, for grace, in her is shown,
A form that peers the lily-wand—
   An air the lily's self might own;
Not such her vaunt, tho' such enchant,
   Nay, make with joy the reason reel,
'Tis hers to bear a boon more rare,—
   A heart another's woe to feel.

Nor hers the hair that beams afar
   Like streams of molten gold—an eye—
That twinkles like the little star
   Attends the virgin moon on high;
Not such her vaunt, yet joy will haunt
   Whoe'er her gentle smile has viewèd;
That smile would light the gloom would blight
   A heart with lion-nerve endued.

Not hers the golden tones that break
   Like music from the lips, the rare—
The dancing dimple on the cheek
   Accorded to the fabled fair;
Not such her vaunt—nay, pride might taunt
   Her with a lack of charms—yet oh!
She's to the faint and weak a saint
   Ordained to bless this world below.

THE CRUSHED ASPIRER.

O, My Spirit, art thou vanquisht?
    Is thy latest prospect gone?
Must my task be thus relinquisht
    Ere my noble end is won?

Must I die, and be remember'd
    Never more, ah, never more!
As the clown who laught and slumber'd
    Out his passing mortal hour?

Has my life been one untiring
    Vigil kept at sorrow's shrine,—
One unceasing toil acquiring
    What unsought for had been mine?

Have I undergone privations
    That the noblest soul had bow'd,—
Stoop to unearn'd degradations
    But to die, as die the crowd?

Whither wilt thou wander? whither?
    From thy quest my soul refrain!
Sure the God who sent me hither
    Had some purpose in my pain.

THE MYSTERIOUS RIDER.

Upon a steed he came with speed,
  The Day behind him breaking;
And still he sped when Day o'erhead
  Her last farewell was taking.

"Ah, whither fliest?—Name thy goal!"
"The Dark from which I bounded!"
He spake and fled; and in my soul,
  The voice night-long resounded.

AN ERROR.

I never said my verse you'd mock'd;
  Nor how you'd giggled at my grammar—
You, on whom Fame her door has lock'd,
  I little mark'd your empty clamour.

I merely said that when you'd call'd
  On Fame, and thrice her cruel porters
Had kick'd you off, thrice back you crawl'd,
  And kiss'd, thrice kiss'd, their hinder-quarters.

BECKY SHARP.

I.

THE DITTY.

O, BECKY SHARP, dear Becky Sharp!
  So very clever and so witty;
I'm half inclined your praise to harp
  In one, at least, well-worded ditty.

First be it sung, You're framed for love —
  "For love, thou fool?" cried Beck, upspringing,
And snatching up the tongs, half clove
  My head, and off "thou fool!" went singing.

II.

CONSOLATION.

SWEET Becky Sharp, sweet Beck, upon
  A time I tried to frame a ditty,
For which you knock'd me down, anon,
  And left me sprawling without pity.

Sir Crawley plus Sir Sprawley, then
  Was I, and yet you little honey,
How charming was't next half-hour, when
  You came and kiss'd away — my money.

III.

THE PRECIOUS PEARL.

Dear Becky Sharp, you lovely girl!
　Come, now on knacks my money's lavished,
I yet have left one precious pearl
　With which your brokers may be ravished.

"Where, Crawley, dear!" Why even here—
　Ah, no; I dream—Sweet mercy, bless us!
I thought I'd yet that manhood, pet,
　I had ere I had thy caresses.

IV.

THE TOAST.

Best Becky Sharp, pray do not carp,
　Nor turn your cherry lip up snarling—
"Man, are you mad?—this Becky bad,
　Why, she's a visionary darling!"

Is't so? "'Tis so!"—Your glasses ring—
　Ring then and toast the bright ideal;
Ah, bring the ideal Beckies, bring!
　And take away the Beckies real!

MISFORTUNE.

Away with the muses of frolic!—away
With the haunts of diversion and folly!—and mine—
Ay, mine be the joy to awaken a lay,
And to weave for misfortune a garland divine.

We shrink at life's shadows and fly to the bowl,
Tho' warned and reminded again and again,
That the death of the reason's the death of the soul,
And what seemeth a loss may in fact be a gain.

Full often to us is the loss or the cross
What the furnace itself's to the nugget of ore;
And the more we are freed from mortality's dross,
The brighter the soul and her glory the more.

The saint is the grander when smitten by woe—
The sinner excites a sweet thrill in our breast;
And still from the presence of sorrow shall flow
What endeareth the spirit by sorrow possest.

Cleopatra of old threw o'er Cæsar a spell,
And her life was a chain of such triumphs, and yet
Her very chief glory began when she fell,
And her blood as a meal to the viper was set.

Not only the victims of virtue we mourn,
    But the victims of error our pity enthral;
And the tear we let fall o'er a Lucretia's urn,
    Leaves a tear o'er the urn of a Helen to fall.

Not alone round the brows of the martyrs of right,
    But a halo encircles the victims of wrong;
And if history's muse in a Hampden delight,
    Not less is a Stuart the Idol of song.

Endeared thro' affliction, thro' anguish endeared,
    By pity to many a vigil is kept,
Who else, with the idols by fashion revered,
    Unmourned in the waters of Lethe had slept.

The mortal immortal becomes upon earth;
    And the spirit thro' trials is helped to the goal,
Where the mantle of glory and girdle of worth,
    Are the meed that awaiteth the tender in soul.

Be our state e'er so lofty, down, down, we must sink,
    When the dire wheel of fortune moves on, as it may,
But the greater the blow sooner broken the link
    By which we are bound to what smacks of the clay.

Then give me the gift to awaken a lay,
    And to weave for misfortune a garland divine;
And the world and its follies may go on their way—
    A rapture unknown to the giddy is mine.

IO PÆAN.

TRIUMPHANT o'er trouble, triumphant o'er pain,
Triumphant o'er all and thro' all we shall hie,
With the cry "Iö Pæan ! and Echo, the strain,
From her cave " Iö Pæan !" enraptured shall cry.

The storm may set in and the summer may go,
But, the while winter winds in the rafters yet roar,
Will a gleam in the cloud and a bloom in the snow,
Give a pledge of a glory-girt future in store.

In Pandora's Box, Hope was left, and, in fact,
As long as the world on its axis shall move,
The Parcæ from mortals will never exact
What a ban, not a boon, in the sequel will prove.

Not only our manfold evils externe,
But the ashes-fill'd apples by error pluck'd, they—
Even they emanate from a fountain superne,
And will prove to be true golden apples one day.

Thro' the regions of Erebus lay the rough road,
By which the brave passed to the Fields of the Blest,
Yet once having enter'd Jove's envied abode,
The trouble made sweeter the pleasure possesst.

Dragon-watched was the idol of Jason's desire,
  Yet a triumph awaited the noble and wise;
And as sure as the faggot but heatens the fire,
  As sure did the danger but brighten the prize.

Creation itself from a chaos was born—
  So sang the Illumed of the centuries fled;
And Atë herself to an Eros would turn,
  If aright the vast drift of existence were read.

Nay, neither the gloom that o'er-shadows our skies,
  Nor the danger that lies on the path to our goal,
Nor the keenest of pangs need awaken our sighs;
  From woe the soul wrings the delight of the soul!

Triumphant o'er trouble, triumphant o'er pain,
  Triumphant o'er all and thro' all we shall hie
With the cry " Iö Pæan ! " and Echo, the strain,
  From her cave " Iö Pæan ! " enraptured shall cry.

LITTLE ANNA.

LITTLE Anna, young and fair,
  How with heart a-dancing,
I descry her image rare,
  O'er the footway glancing;
Ah, those locks of dusky hue,
  Ah, those eyes that twinkle,
Now I laugh their sheen to view,
  Now my tears down trinkle.

Chorus—Well-a-way, night and day,
    I must sigh; nor can a
  Youth once view her charms, 1.
    rue
  The peerless charms of Anna!

When I see her bonny blink,
  I'm upraised to heaven;
When upon her ways I think,
  From myself I'm driven;
Not a bit of use am I,
  Save with arms a-kimbo,
Thus to sit and thus to sigh,
  A very wretch in limbo.

Chorus—Well-a-way, etc.

Up, from tossings, to and fro,
  Bite or sup unheeded,
Up from bed to work I go,
  Long before 'tis needed;
But a-pit, love a-smit,
  Do all I can do, now,
Still a-wry the pick will fly,
  And no coal will hew, now.

Chorus—Well a-way, etc.

Can it be her voice I hear,
  When my pick is swinging?
When her tongue attracts the ear
  Golden bells are ringing;
Do I dream? or is't her e'en
  Yonder nook adorning?
Blacker than the coal, their sheen
  Mocks the coal a burning!

Chorus—Well-a-way, etc.

Ah those locks and ah, those eyes,
  Ah, the rest they've broken;
But in vain their victim tries—
  Love can ne'er be spoken;
Man may fathom ocean—say
  The reason of its motion;
But love's magic never! nay
  'Tis deeper than the ocean.

Chorus—Well-a-way, etc.

CRUEL ANNA.

Little Anna, cruel elf,
  Spite of all my reason,
She yet puts me from myself
  In and out of season;
Ah, the may, ah, the fay,
  Glee to mischief wedded!
Foe to rest, she's a pest,
  And always to be dreaded!

  Chorus—Ah, the may, ah, the fay—
      Glee to mischief wedded!
      Foe to rest, she's a pest—
      And always to be dreaded!

Never goes the sun around,
  But upon me stealing,
She, she doth my soul confound,
  Sends my reason reeling;
Gars me sing, and while, alack,
  I in glee am singing,
On me turns and in a crack,
  Gives my ear a-wringing.

  Chorus—Ah, the may, etc.

Pat she comes and goes, the wasp!
  Back anon she hummeth;
Round my neck her hands to clasp,
  That to do she cometh;
So she leads me to suppose
  By her air entrancing,
Till I'm twitted by the nose
  And again sent dancing.

  Chorus—Ah, the may, etc.

Ear or nose, or wrung or stung,
  'Tween a thumb and finger,
How to be avenged now long
  Lost in doubt I linger;
Then when I resolved at last
  Rush her pride to humble;
Lo, o'er me a glamour cast,
  O'er the stools I tumble.

  Chorus—Ah, the may, etc.

Head-a-turned, heart-a-burned,
  Nay reduced to cinders;
Nose-a-stung, ears-a-wrung,
  Shins all sent to flinders;
Pale and thin, bone and skin—
  I'm a spectre merely;
And he who'd play my part might say
  He'd bought his whistle dearly.

  Chorus—Ah, the may, etc.

BALOO.

Baloo, my sweet baby—the blossom !
    I dandle't till weary, and sigh,
With not a bare drop in my bosom
    To silence its pitiful cry.

The red moon above us right rarely,
    I lay on the brink of the burn,
And drank in the words which so early
    Have brought me to anguish and scorn.

And had he but thought of the trouble,
    And had he but thought on the pain :
Tho' green in the blade with the stubble,
    I'm fated to bleach on the plain.

Mid all our wooed maidens so many,
    The bonny bright lily was I ;
But now plucked and tainted, like any
    Vile weed on the footway I lie.

But let anguish thus my heart rend, and
    The briny tear thus my cheek lave ;
The longest lane yet has an end, and
    The weary sleep sound in the grave.

Baloo, my sweet baby—the blossom !—
    Ah ! hush—ere his life-glass is run,
The false one shall find in his bosom
    A pang for the deed he has done.

THE RUIN.

The bitter wind blows o'er the desolate wold,
  —The bloom from the blossom forever is sped!—
And I must trudge on thro' the sleet and the cold,
  And sweet to my heart were the lot of the dead.

Upon my shrunk bosom sleep seizeth my child,
  —The bloom from the blossom forever is sped!—
Awaken my darling!—Alas, I'm beguiled,
  And would I too slept the sound sleep of the dead.

Cold, cold are its feet and its bosom, and oh,
  —The bloom from the blossom forever is sped!—
No more will the bird prove a light to my woe;
  And would I too slept the sound sleep of the dead.

Its sweet glossy eyes seem to look at me yet,
  —The bloom from the blossom forever is sped!—
They mind me of others I fain would forget;
  And would I too slept the sound sleep of the dead.

Its soft silken locks, e'er as sunny as soft,
  —The bloom from the blossom forever is sped!—
A-wet are the curlies I've kissed so oft;
  And would I too slept the sound sleep of the dead.

The wee tottie crept atween me and my toil,
  —The bloom from the blossom forever is sped !—
But then its bit smile had the trick of his smile,
  And would that I slept the sound sleep of the dead.

No father had I once to threaten or frown,
  —The bloom from the blossom forever is sped !—
And mother kept silent till reason had flown,
  Then dropt she to sleep—the sound sleep of the dead.

I've reached the old ruin endeared by the past,
  —The bloom from the blossom forever is sped !—
He'll come here and find our bones whiten'd at last,
  And lie down and rest by the dust of the dead.

LIFE AND DEATH.

Oh, what is Life ? A magic night
  In which we still to phantoms yield ;
And what is Death, if not the light
  By which the real truth's reveal'd ?

THE SUMMER BREEZELET.

"Not now shall I sing of my sports in Spring,
    But the golden hours and gay,"
Sang the Breeze, "when I, a wild lover, hie
    With the Summer flowers to play.

"When I tiptoe go to the pansy, tho'
    She wag to and fro her head,
She yet likes, I know, my kisses, and so
    Is kist on her low green bed.

"The rose newly born, albeit she's sworn
    Her lover shall mourn, I woo,
And escape untorn by her pointed thorn,
    And never a scorn may rue.

"The pink she may shrink at my touch, I think,
    When her sweets I drink in glee,
At the theft she'll wink, and a kindly blink,
    Will the sweet-mouth'd pink throw me.

"That snowy white may, the lily I sway,
    And when I essay, love stirred,
In my own wild way with the saint to play,
    No cruel Nay is heard.

ALAS!

"When I in my zeal to the poppy steal,
  Tho' she'd fain conceal her flame,
Yet she'll rock and reel with feeling I feel,
  Nor seek my zeal to blame.

"The woodbine too—nay, all blooms I woo
  In the fields or bowers, and O,
And the mad pranks we will play, and the glee,
  And the golden hours, we know!"

———

ALAS!

Alas! the woe the high of heart,
  Seem pre-ordained to undergo,
While proud ambition hides the smart,
  And smiles delude the world below.

Their anguish, like a Samson blind,
  Gropes on in darkness, till at length
It grasps the pillars of the mind,
  And dies a victim to its strength.

LOTTY HAY.

As I came down from Earsdon Town,
    A-lilting of a lay,
Whom did I meet but she, the sweet,
    The blue-eyed Lotty Hay.

A crimson blush her cheek did flush,
    Nor sin did that betray;
The pearl is sure a jewel pure,
    And so is Lotty Hay.

All evil flees her heart, yet she's
    To Slander's shafts a prey,
And words of ill do nearly kill
    The lowly Lotty Hay.

Some deem her proud; in speech aloud
    Some other mays will say
She's cold or fierce, and all to pierce
    The heart of Lotty Hay.

Proud?—She's not proud: to-day I view'd
    An ant beside her stray,
And that wee thing kind blinks did bring
    From soft eyed Lotty Hay.

Fierce?—She's not fierce; a fly did pierce—
  Late pierce her bosom—yea,
And made her cry, yet that bad fly
  Was spared by Lotty Hay.

Not proud nor bold, not fierce nor cold,
  But meek, kind, mild alway—
A soul of light did meet my sight
  As I pass'd Lotty Hay.

Upon her way she went and, nay,
  Not lighter moved to-day
The thistle-down then upward flown,
  Than walked this Lotty Hay.

In cotton gown she tript to town,
  And not a lady gay
In satin drest could be more blest
  Than seemed sweet Lotty Hay.

DOLLY DARE.

AT Backworth sung till echo rung,
  A bard whose feelings were,
In what to young and old he sung
  Of little Dolly Dare.

" Tho' Lizzy's sweet and Polly's neat,
  And Fanny she is fair,
There's truly none, was never one,
  So blithe as Dolly Dare.

In doors and out she stirs about
  As if she felt aware,
By labour glows more red the rose
  That dowereth Dolly Dare.

A duty here with forehead clear,
  With grace a duty there,
She'll do, and do what very few
  Can do, will Dolly Dare.

She, knitting, will a ditty trill ;
  And, to an olden air,
The needles bright dance left and right
  Of sweet-tongued Dolly Dare.

Beneath her touch, its power is such,
  As bright as palace rare,
The cottage seems, and in it gleams
  A Queen in Dolly Dare.

The pots and mugs and pans and jugs
    Into their places fare,
And clearer glow and dearer grow
    When touched by Dolly Dare.

The bread she bakes, the beds she makes,
    And up and down the stair,
On tripping toe will dancing go
    The tidy Dolly Dare.

To words of mirth she scours the hearth,
    While in his easy chair
Old Robin lies and, smoking, eyes
    With pride his Dolly Dare.

Her pail to fill she'll to the rill,
    Or to the well, and there
Doth clearly see Truth's self, for she
    Therein sees Dolly Dare.

'Tis thus away she'll while the day,
    And then to me repair,
When envy smit the moments flit
    O'er me and Dolly Dare."

The bard his song so sung and long,
    Tho' plain his verses were,
Wagg'd every tongue with what he sung
    Of little Dolly Dare.

LILLY AND WILLY.

If Ellerton Willy be slighted by Lilly !
Yet others as bonny will hark to his lay ;
Then why like a silly bit daffodowndilly,
Should I droop my head, droop, and cry, well-a-way?

Chorus :—Then why should pine Willy ? if slighted by Lilly,
Yet others as bonny will hark to his lay, etc.

Has Effie, a violet sweet, and a sweeter
In Wanie's fair valley ne'er lifted its head,
Not pined hour by hour since I promised to meet her,
And met with this music-tongued Lilly instead ?

Chorus :—Then why should pine Willy ? etc.

Has Tibbie, the pride of the Moor, and whose glances
Are spells that enrapture the young and the old,
—The Queen of our dancers, so finely she dances—
Not sighed for the love at which Lilly is cold ?

Chorus :—Then why should pine Willy ? etc.

Has Meg, at whose bearing the Hirsts are enchanted,
  And whom as a charmer the charmer respects,
Not tipt me the wink, and thrice hinted if wanted,
  She'd skip at the proffer this Lilly rejects?

Chorus:—Then why should pine Willy? etc.

Would Clara herself, at whose dimples and madly
  Young Robin of Uffam would dance in delight,
Not slip a red-rose in her hair and hie gladly
  To wile, could she wile, me from Lilly to night?

Chorus:—Then why should pine Willy? if slighted by
    Lilly,
  Yet others as bonny will hark to his lay,
Then why like a silly bit daffodowndilly,
  Should I droop my head, droop, and cry,
    well-a-way?

BARBARA BELL.

A new song to an old tune.

Away to the pic-nic at Ryton, away
Went off in the sunrise our younkers pell-mell—
And many were bonny and many were gay,
But sweetest of any was Barbara Bell.

Chorus:—As sweet as a cherry was Barbara Bell,
Both tricksy and merry was Barbara Bell;
Tho' others that day were bonny and gay—
The Queen of the charmers was Barbara Bell.

Nan Harley was there, her locks in the sun
Did sparkle and burn, yet woful to tell,
No spoils by her long yellow tresses were won—
The lads only hankered for Barbara Bell.

Chorus:—As sweet as a cherry was Barbara Bell, etc.

Meg Wilson came up, her eyes black as jet—
And tho' at a fair oft ruled by their spell,
Meg fail'd even one rosy apple to get—
No pickings were there but for Barbara Bell.

Chorus:—As sweet as a cherry was Barbara Bell, etc.

BARBARA BELL.

Nell Dowey appeared, in her dimples adorned,
  The rose of the roses was she on the Fell ;
But somehow this rose to a daffodil turn'd
  That moment she glided near Barbara Bell.

Chorus :—As sweet as a cherry was Barbara Bell, etc.

The lovely and young, they danced and they sung,
  Till down came the night and darkened the dell ;
When homeward they hied—a star for their guide—
  And who was that star saving Barbara Bell !

Chorus :—As sweet as a cherry was Barbara Bell,
  Both tricksy and merry was Barbara Bell,
Tho' others that day were bonny and gay
  The Queen of the charmers was Barbara Bell.

THE DEATH OF CLEOPATRA.

I go—from all earth can give, riven
   By fate's sternest mandate—so—so,
A Queen in a fiery car driven,
   To meet her god-lover—I go.

That blissful reunion to hasten,
   Hie, hie, with the worm to my breast;
And here let its fatal lips fasten—
   On here where a god's head would rest.

Here, here let it suck and be suckled,
   On what hath this pallid cheek dyed,
When on his fell weapon I've buckled,
   And frolic-mad mimick'd his stride.

That golden day's vanished, yet, clingeth
   One hope to the fallen one,—nay,
A lay in the murky cloud ringeth,
   And dances her heart at that lay.

"Even yet will she meet with his olden
   Blink" rings that sweet music;—"her love,
Whose smile will make Hades more golden
   Than Jove's gilded palace above.

"Even yet will she thrill with the glory
  That stream from his looks, as she'd thrill;
And hear from his tongue the sweet story
  Of what she once was—and is still!

"A Queen is she not, who o'er victors,
  A victor hath trodden, while Kings
Would smile on her prætors and lictors,
  And gift their attendants with rings?

"And so in the far future ages,
  Some poet will chant to the throng;
And Rulers, and Heroes, and Sages,
  An echo return to the song.

"Then spirits Titanic shall wonder
  At one who o'er nations would reign,
As if the dread bolt of the thunder
  Had danced in delight in her train.

"As if Jove himself had forbidden
  All ill thro' her portals to tread,
And here would on lightning have ridden
  To save a small hair of her head.

"A god-guarded women, they'll hold her;
  A god-illumed soul—and aright!
Ay, where were the eyes could behold her,
  And not in her glory delight?

"Her graces a Pompey would dazzle;
   A Cæsar his faulchion would sheath,
Their vassal to be—and their vassal
   Shall now be the victor-king—Death.

"Her body will perish, but rarer
   The spirit that gilds it will gleam,
And to her own Marcus yet fairer
   Whatever seemed fairest, will seem.

"The sun-soaring bird afire flashes
   A wreck to the wonder-bound earth;
But up the next hour from its ashes,
   Again the sun-scaler goes forth.

"A Phœnix the Phœnix succeedeth;
   So up from the dust doth she spring,
And go in a lustre that feedeth
   With rapture the eyes of her King.

"His star, from his burnished throne yonder,
   He sees, as he saw her of old,
A-far on the Cydnus—a wonder,
   That turns the black Styx into gold.

"And hers he is still."—Thro' my anguish,
   Thus rings that sweet voice in my ears:
And not in her sorrows may languish
   The soul which such harmony hears.

That voice, at its sound I'm uplifted,
  Nor feel as I've felt, weak and worn ;
That voice at its music I'm gifted
  With strength yet the foeman to scorn.

The Roman may giggle, the Roman
  May sound his brass timbrels in mirth ;
Shall he make a mock of the woman
  Erewhile the delight of the earth ?

Shall she to the seven-hilled City
  In triumph be hurried in deed ?
No, no, from their laughter or pity,
  Ah, see by the viper she's freed.

Freed, free is her spirit and given
  Power—"longings immortal"—and oh !—
A Queen in a fiery car driven
  To meet her god-lover, I go.

THE CHARMER.

A song in devotion I sing to my Annie—
  Ah! be startled not to discover I long
To fold in my arms and possess what so many
  And many a time is the theme of my song.

My manhood's dissolved at the sight of thy beauty,
  And while heart can feel and such beauty is known,
What youth could be kept by a mere sense of duty
  From yearning to call the enchanter his own?

The saint he may blame—so to do is the fashion—
  And carp at my feelings and call them a sin;
Could beauty like thine be the price of his passion,
  He'd rush to perdition the jewel to win.

To view thy locks blacker than coal and thy glances;
  To hear thy voice, sweetest of music—ay, ay—
Thy manifold beauty my spirit entrances,
  And reason deserts me when Annie is nigh!

THE BROKEN SPELL.

Come sing me the song that once gilded my gloom,
    And the heart unsubdued till that moment subdued,
That with its red rose caused the rose-tree to bloom,
    That long year after year without blossoms had stood.

With thy hand on my hand, and thy cheek by my cheek,
    In thy wild and weird tones, be that lay again sung,
And the bleak world to me, shall no longer be bleak,
    And this heart, wrung by anguish, no longer be wrung.

Then over thy grace, shall thy voice throw a grace ;
    And that image which long had its home in my breast,
Be robed in a splendour, no pencil could trace,
    And possest of a charm by no other possest.

Than its red, shall thy lip then a richer dye show,
    And with beams brighter still, shall thy hazel eyes burn ;
And thy beauty, deep down in my spirit, shall glow,
    And my life to a drop of pure ecstasy turn.

Shall the boon then be mine? shall that music reward
    Thus the faith of a heart that yet leapt at its strain?
Ah, broken's the spell of that song I oft heard,
    And so—so thro' thy dark guile to me shall remain.

THE FAIRIES' ADIEU.

Our revels now are ended, so good night, so good night,
    And each unto our chamber let us hie,
And there lose ourselves in visions till the broad daylight
    Again has bid adieu unto the sky.
        So good-bye
    Till day has gone out of the sky.

"My couch is in the daisy with its golden, golden eye,"
"And mine is in the violet, sweet and pure,"
"And mine the modest blue bell, beneath whose canopy
    I dream away the angry day secure."
        So good-bye
    Till day has gone out of the sky.

But when the day's departed, upstarting from our dreams
    We'll gather in a ring upon the green,
And there dance till night's enraptured, and the pale moon
      seems
    To mourn the fate that changeth such a scene.
        So good-bye
    Till day has gone out of the sky.

The Magic Glass.

I.

THE INNER HARP.

The memories of moments flown,
   Into my spirit's glass assemble;
And as they enter, one by one,
   My heart-strings into music tremble.

Even as the harp, the breezelet sways,
   So thrills my heart responsive ever
Unto the thoughts of other days
   That came and went—and went forever!

II.

THE FAIR ROWER.

She took the oars and rowed along
   With such a grace, the mere did waken
Into a sweet, melodious song,
   At every charming stroke was taken.

And at each sound, the hills around,
   By many a magic memory haunted,
And skies did seem with joy to gleam
   Within the mere, her strokes enchanted.

III.

THE LUCKY HOUR.

The fickle Moon has left the skies;
But Night's blue veil with stars is sprinkled,
And every little twinkler tries
　　To twinkle as he'd never twinkled.

O, now's the hour for Love to pour,
　　And Beauty hear his vows supernal;
No Moon will glint of change to hint,
　　And stars but hint of things eternal.

IV.

THE ASSURANCE.

Ah dearest dear, what do I hear?
　　I've hurt thy feelings! have I, dearest?
Then let thy words be fiery swords,
　　To punish me with pangs severest!

Than hear thee sigh, I'd rather die;
　　Ay, were Death's gruesome terrors doubled,—
I'd rather die than hear thee sigh,
　　Or deem thy heart a moment troubled

V.

THE SECRET.

The wind comes from the west to-night;
  So sweetly down the lane he bloweth
Upon my lips, with pure delight,
  From head to foot my body gloweth.

Where did the wind, the magic find
  To charm me thus? say, heart that knoweth!
"Within a rose on which he blows
  Before upon thy lips he bloweth!"

VI.

THE BUGLE-HORN.

O, the bugle-horn I heard last night!
  Its wild tones set the echoes flying;
And night long in my soul, Delight
  Danced, danced her gift for dancing trying!

Such tones, I swear a magic bear,
  Which turns to heaven the hell man mourneth,
And almost match the joys I snatch,
  When Minnie's rose my breast adorneth!

VII.

THE PEARL.

Unknit that brow; the day too soon
    Departs when starry nights are nearer;
They're clouded now, nor will the Moon
    Once come and try to make them clearer.

Be not like her, a peevish girl;—
    I own I err'd; but when I dearer
Than worlds appraised thy rival's pearl—
    I only meant that pearl, its wearer!

VIII.

THE TWO-FOLD SURPRISE.

She snapt her fingers, on her heel,
    Her sweet boot-heel, she turned and left me;
What did I feel?—What could I feel,
    At what of paradise had reft me?

I swooning lay; my soul away
    To hell had fled, by madness driven—
Where—where!—she met again the pet,
    Who'd come to coax her back to—heaven!

IX.

THE RETURN.

Can this be her? Her dark eyes show
Two planets in the midnight heaven;
Her cheeks the blood-rose—her brow
The snow upon the mountains driven;

Her tongue's a silver bell to hear,
Ah, death when certain words are spoken!—
Can this be her? And comes the dear
To break again the heart she's broken?

X.

THE BEE AND THE ROSE.

"You wont!" the Rose's accents ring;
"I will!" the Golden Bee's are ringing;
And tho' the winds, to aid her, spring,
Soon with the breeze-tost bloom he's swinging.

His prize secured, away he goes,
At which anon, in rage the rarest;
"Come back thou villain!" cries the Rose;
"Come once more kiss me, if thou darest!"

XI.

THE ROSE'S COMPLAINT.

"You naughty Bee!" the Red Rose said;
"To come at noon by Envy driven,
And wound the bloom whose beauty made
The Sun to linger in the heaven!

"I little dream'd, while I did grant
An ear unto one little story,
You'd meed with stings, for what to vaunt
You Golden Sun had given his glory!"

XII.

THE ECHO.

"Adieu!" she cried, and with that cry
Adown the star-lit valley fleeted,
And Echo from her tower on high,
With cruel tongue, the word repeated.

"What?—Never!" cried I, yet possess'd
Of hope, that by some sweet endeavour,
Again we'd meet our hearts at rest,
When—"What?" cried startled Echo;—"Never!"

XIII.

THE MINSTREL.

Ah, deem not when thy minstrel tunes
   His harp to hours and glories vanished,
His star of stars, his moon of moons,
   Can ever from his heart be banish'd.

Each tune he wakes, each note that takes
   And charms the heart, Love's arrow woundeth,
But flows from strings she only rings,
   And from a Deep, she only soundeth.

XIV.

THE SEEN AND THE UNSEEN.

They cry, "How light, the heart and bright,
   From which proceed such strains of gladness!"
They can't discern the pangs that burn,
   And seek to drive the bard to madness.

From pryers vain, he hides his pain,
   And while with skill his harp he's plying,
They mark the bloom upon the tomb,
   But not the ruin in it lying!

XV.

THE FAIR THIEF.

THE rogue, she smiled, then swept away,
   Her raven locks behind her streaming;
My very pulse forgot to play,
   And I was left in wonder dreaming.

The Pleiads lost their charms that night;
   And Dian lost her bow and quiver;
They'd with the damsel taken flight,
   And never have been found since—never!

XVI.

THE TWO MIRRORS.

SHE took the wood thro' which she sung,
   But in the lake near which she wended,
An image met, and swayed and swung,
   And three times with her image blended.

The vision from that mirror fled,
   But, ah! I found when day had vanish'd,
It only to a glass had sped,
   From which it never can be banish'd.

XVII.

THE ONE SOLACE.

I MIGHT have wish'd it otherwise;
 But yet, poor heart, tho' they were cruel —
Those thunder-clouds above her eyes,
 They very much became the jewel!

Hope fled, but Truth remains, and owns
 What yet this fond heart half-beguileth;
"One knows the worst on't when she frowns,
 But never when the syren smileth!"

XVIII.

THE SYREN.

HER harp she takes, from string to string,
 Her little snowy fingers, glancing,
Into Night's ear a wild spell fling,
 And all the while my heart is dancing.

Why thus, fond heart, thus dancest thou?
 "A dream of old in memory lingers,
At thought of which I dance to know
 That mine are not the strings she fingers!"

XIX.

THE CLOUD.

A CLOUD the valley domes, and down
　　Yon erewhile sun-lit mountain stealeth,
And bit by bit, with one black frown,
　　The green and gold below concealeth.

Down, down it comes, and pain me numbs,
　　To think how soon yon vision splendid—
Yon one last scene of gold and green,
　　Must like my other dreams have ended.

XX.

THE SONGSTRESS.

BACK flies my soul to other years,
　　When thou that charming lay repeatest,
When smiles were only chased by tears,
　　Yet sweeter far than smiles the sweetest.

Thy music ends, and where are they?
　　Those golden times by memory cherish'd?
O, syren, sing no more that lay
　　Or sing till I like them have perish'd!

1886.

The Golden Bowl.

I.

THE BOWL.

Just let the Owl of Evil howl;
    To mourners of each rank and station,
I cry, Come, troll the Golden Bowl!
    And quaff me with a deep potation.

Each sparkling droplet to the soul
    Will yield o'er Care a bright ovation;
Then seize and troll the Golden Bowl!
    That beams—in my imagination.

II.

THE RIGHT THING.

When Day once stirs, her locks of gold,
    Up, seize, ere she is well awaken!
And with her steps thy paces hold,
    Till she from Earth her leave hath taken.

What tho' upon the way she frown,
    Her goal attained, unto thee turning,
With such a gift thy toil she'll crown,
    Thou'lt thank her with a smile next morning!

III.

THE TOWER.

My wee, wee fawn, you see me yawn?
Well, I'm not much disposed to flattery;
And were I so, you rogue! you know
    You're proof against the fiercest battery.

You have an ear? of stone, my dear;
    A heart? yes, yes, of temper'd iron,
And love of self, the little elf,
    Doth with a Tower of Brass environ!

IV.

TOO TRUE.

Truth's words are oft so very true—
    And always when my lips he uses,
His foes, which let us hope, are few,
    Declare he but the truth abuses.

Thus when he spake of Ella's tongue,
    She knew he meant the tongue of Fable;
And when of her sweet deeds he sung,—
    She kick'd his shins beneath the table.

V.

NOT JEALOUS.

"I JEALOUS ?   Pooh !—Doth not her eyes
   Pursue his vessel o'er the billows ?
No, jealous, no !—From whence those sighs ?"
   —'Tis but the wind among the willows !

"Ha, jealous, ha !—Did darling speak ?
   What said my chuck ?—La, I'm not jealous !"
"—Did Jack say he'd return next week ?"
   " What ? Wench ? Go hang those sailor fellows ! '

VI.

JACK THE ROVER.

" My brother Jack the Rover, Sir !"
   " Bless me, I thought he was a cousin ?"
" Bound on a voyage to Elsinore ! "
   " Most merry damsels have a dozen !"

"That wench you tackled up the street ?"
   " My sister Ciss ?   My loving sister ?"
" Just as I thought—she looked so sweet,—
   And you yet sweeter,—as you kissed her ! "

VII.

EXTREME KINDNESS.

When I would laugh a little at
　　The follies that in Life aboundeth,
What ails the saint I worship, that
　　She with a frown my spirit woundeth?

Is laughter sin? ah, then full well
　　I see she'd here but curb my laughter,
And steep me in the heart of hell,
　　To save me from its lips hereafter.

VIII.

STEEDS AND THEIR RIDERS.

Don't spur us so: you'll ever find,
　　When you will ride at giddy paces
There's always something in the wind,
　　At which ere long you'll twist your faces.

What, we're but steeds whom no one recks?
　　Then spurs us till we're sores all over:
The sooner you have smash'd your necks,
　　The sooner we'll have gone to clover!

IX.

UNCOUTH THINGS.

"I HATE outlandish things, and own
    I've little liking for the sonnet;
'Tis for a lazy Muse, and one
    Who hath a bumler in her bonnet.

"'Tis a humdrum song, and tho' not long,
    I'd sooner be a kitten, sooner,
And 'Mew!' cry 'Mew!' than listen to
    The ordinary sonnet crooner!"

X.

WHAT ELSE?

"You little like the sonnet? *You?*
    But what are you? a creaking wicket;
A cricket in the grass, allow
    Me, slut! to say a very cricket!—

"A chatter-box, or at the best"—
    "'A win-chat,' add, and end the matter!"
"Not so, slut Muse!—You're tongue's a pest,
    And"—"La, what can it do but clatter?"

XI.

HAG NIGHT.

La, what a Night! The hag has sworn,
    In hue to prove a chimla sweeper;
And did the North not blow his horn,
    No star would dare to show its peeper.

How black her look!—(Just like the rook,
    That on my idol's brow appeareth,
When quite o'ercome with wrath she's dumb,
    And not a blink her booby cheereth!)

XII.

JUST THE WAY.

Was ever wretch in such a plight?
    I scramble on I know not whither!
The witches are abroad to-night;
    Some wicked one has led me hither!

"That's just like you, you'll have your cue,
    And when hood-wink'd you kiss the ditches,
Your hair you tear! your Muse forswear!
    And blame and ban the wicked witches!"

XIII.

THE WITCH-GLASS.

A SYREN, with her mirror bright,
　His ear enchants ; and while he listens,
His image on his dazzled sight,
　A very jewel gleams and glistens.

Ah, could he peer into yon brook,
　Or into any heart that knows him,
He'd find the thing that met his look,
　Was not the pearl the Witch-Glass shows him !

XIV.

NOT THE BIRD.

HE's not the bird I took him for—
　I heard him in the distance screaming,
And tho' his voice was harsh, that hour,
　I dream'd of glories, golden, gleaming !

This hour he meets my closer view ;
　And tho' he cuts as big a swagger,
I find a little cockatoo,
　And not a peacock, in the bragger !

XV.

DAME MALICE.

DAME Malice reigns the Queen of hags;
   With wink and whisper, nod and chatter,
She trots along, and never fags,
   While she has scandal-seeds to scatter.

Then when her seeds are poison-weeds,
   That choke the corn and spoil the labors
Of king or clown, her feats to crown,
   She'll dance a reelet with her neighbors!

XVI.

RUMOUR.

ELF Rumour? Ay, the airy fay,
   That treads the air unseen by any;
From town to town, her bugle's blown,
   And merry are her pranks, and many.

Her news our ears now charm, our fears
   Now stir, as with a clap of thunder,
And while we cry out, What? she'll fly,
   With Laughter at her heels, and Wonder.

XVII.

THE CRITICS.

I LIKE the darling critics—like?
O, how upon their work I linger,
When they their weapons use to strike,
Not me, but some less happy singer.

The treasure of their venom-bags
So finely on the bard's expended,
One half-forgets the little wags
Were from a scorpion-race descended!

XVIII.

THE PETITION.

DEAR critics, pray, what have I done
That thus you frown so? tell me truly?
"You've for your neck a halter spun,
In blaming of our race unduly!"

Don't hang me, pray!—Just praise my lay,
And I will swear the Muse but garbled
My sweet intent; and what was meant
Was not the blame the Gipsy warbled!

XIX.

BILLY TAYLOR.

"Sweet Billy Taylor went to sea!"
 Bravo, my metre ballad-monger!
"With silver buckles on his knee!"
 Another stave—a little longer!

"When he comes back he'll marry me!"
 He'll marry you, you empty, airy
Nothing—marry you? Why, he——
 "'Whoo-hoo!' take that for your vagary!"

XX.

JUST SO.

Just let the Owl of Evil howl!
 To mourners of each rank and station,
I cry, Come troll the Golden Bowl,
 And quaff with me one deep potation!

Each sparkling droplet to the soul
 Will yield o'er care a bright ovation;
Then seize and troll the Golden Bowl,
 That beams—in my imagination!

1886.

The Posy-Gift.

I.

You quite mistake the sprite you chase—
   I'm of the under, not the upper,
Order of the fairy race;
   And cannot go with you to supper.

" You silly elf, Titania's self
   Will"—Tut, be there? My mirth she quenches—
And her stiff airs kick me down-stairs
   To my dear kitchen cats and wenches.

II.

He giggled at the thought, and had
   He been a dog his tail he'd wriggled,
He was at heart so very glad
   At what the little giggler giggled.

" You giggled? Why? Your thought I'd buy—
   The price?" O'er such we've never higgled;
Tis but to task yourself to ask
   At what the little giggler giggled.

III.

ANOTHER stave I'll never rave
  Against the rich folk and their riches;
The men, you knave! are good and brave!
  The women are the sweetest witches!

"What's up now?" Pooh! what's that to you?
  One cannot have a little lunar
Fit, but some one cries out "Mum!"
  And puts the pipe out of the crooner.

IV.

HA, ha! last night I served you right;
  The kick I gave—but I was sorry
I gave it you—but come and view
  What will allay your wrath and worry.

"That posy gay? Well, I dare say—
  Who gave it you? A lady?" Truly!
"What lady, pray?" That I will say,
  When you have learned your manners duly.

V.

These jewels left her very hand ;
  Were pull'd within her very bowers;
Smell, senseless villain ! smell them and
  Say didst thou ever smell such flowers?

"Such flowers ?" the fellow seized his hat—
  "Such flowers ?" he answer'd in derision ;
"Well, I've heard questions strange, but that—
  I'd better run for—a physician ! "

VI.

Come, pretty flowers, and drink my tears;
  'Tis well my better reason chided,
Or I had box'd the rascal's ears,
  That so the little dears derided !

My ruth, not ire, the wretch demands ;
  The magic every cup adorning,
How could he feel ?—saw he the hands
  That placed them into mine this morning?

VII.

What fancies throng into the mind,
    When one upon this posy gazeth;
The more I look, the more I find
    Some semblance that one's ken amazeth.

"What semblance, man? to what? to whom?"
    Go, lack-a-brain, and sweep the stable;
A wooden head must not presume
    To chatter at the Muse's Table!

VIII.

One fancy kicks another's heel;
    But let us seize one while it trembles
In act to fly, and make't reveal
    Wherein each bloom her charms resembles.

These violets blue, not filled with dew,
    But with my tears—are not these weepers—
"What would you say? her eyes are grey,
    And never flash'd two merrier peepers!"

IX.

Once more, sweet Muse, a fancy choose ;
　Seize by the heels that winged fellow—
And he'll declare how this her hair—
　" Her hair is brown, that broom is yellow ! "

Then that one try, I know he'll cry
　This bean-bloom's like her lips.　" Sweet booby !
That runner's quite a scarlet bright,
　Thy lady's lips are very ruby."

X.

Go, Musie, go ! you like, I know,
　To throw a glamour o'er my vision ;
And I but want the truth to chant,
　And Truth shall do it with precision !

He'll not aver this rose-bloom's her,
　This lily-bell, he knows not whether,
But he will tell she's lily-bell
　And red, red rose-bloom, both together !

XI.

These flowers that so reflect the grace
  Of one who is the Queen of Graces!
I'll pop into my richest vase,
  Where I may watch their pretty faces.

And should a fly approach their lips,
  Then, Mercy, shield the little sinner;
For if I catch him on the hips,
  He'll never need another dinner!

XII.

All things of beauty seek to draw
  Unto themselves like things of beauty
In homage to an inner law,
  And which to own's their bounden duty.

So deems my nose—this beauteous nose!
  That out of love, not adulation,
So oft, before this wall-flower, bows,—
  Or homage yields to this carnation.

XIII.

Come, let me smell thee, lily-bell;
  Another smell, my silver lily!
And thou, sweet rose, come to my nose—
  Ah, whence those feelings, soft and silly?

She smell'd you so? the lady? No?
  I know she did; her charming nosy
Drew nectar up from every cup,
  Before she handed me the posy!

XIV.

These lovely blooms, their rich perfumes,
  And many colours, rich and glorious,
My soul illume, o'er care and gloom
  To move a king—a king victorious!

To me things seem, as in a stream,
  Or on the person of my idol,
To wear a sheen before unseen,
  E'en by the gifted bard of Rydal!

XV.

BLIND as the wretch who mock'd my flowers;
    Or rather mock'd their well-won praises,
And swore what came from Eden-bowers,
    Were only buttercups and daisies—

As blind was I till—till—A hare!
    The thought is off, nor can I win it
Back to—well, to—I declare
    This song must end with nothing in it!

XVI.

O, DEAR, dear, dear! what shall I do?
    My only thoughts are off, that clearly
Might have express'd the praises due
    To one I prize, and prize so dearly!

The wine has vanished, and the lees
    To serve up these, would leave one, undone,
Not of the flock of chick-a-dees,
    That chirrup to the folk of London.

XVII.

"HA, ha! at last you're fetter'd fast—
  Was ever such a daft, gigantic
Zany known on earth, or one
  So much the sport of passions frantic?

You kicked me off, with scorn and scoff,
  Then quite ignored the Muse romantic's
Aid, Dame's brow to crown—and now
  You pay the piper for your antics!"

XVIII.

"WITH Common Sense one might dispense,
  But from the Muse's Table surely
To drive away the merry fay,
  The Muse herself, is madness purely?

Then when we dine and drink our wine,
  To have served up Truth's pungent salad's
Enough to make one's nerves to shake
  Whene'er we'd meet our Bag of Ballads!"

XIX.

'Tis quite a treat, as singer knows,
    To have to own one's fairly beaten,
And council's held among the crows
    To learn how soon one may be eaten.

The sparrow-hawks are on the wing—
    The magpies, too, in chorus chatter,
And owlets lend their aid to ring
    The death-bell of——But that's no matter!

XX.

My Song must end; and now I'll send
    It to the critics with this letter:
"Sir, praise this song, and I'm your friend—
    Or if you'd rather——You had better!"

One to my lady fair also
    I'll write, and from the subject borrow
Such fire, that I'll receive, I know,
    Another posy-gift to-morrow.

1886.

A CRY FOR POLAND.

How long shall injustice prevail?
How long shall the weak rue the strong?
The children of Poland bewail
The yoke of the Russian?—How long?
Lo! one generation goes by,
And another succeeds as of old,
Yet no liberation is nigh—
Yet theirs are afflictions untold.
The hero, whose lustre and worth,
Might add to his nation's renown,
Still seeks at a far foreign hearth,
The shelter denied at his own.
No star left her home to illume,
The mother heart-broken and lorn—
The mother looks round on her gloom,
And curses the hour she was born.
In sight of the husband, or sire,
The wife or the daughter's defiled;
And to quench a demoniac ire,
Both mercy and love are reviled.
The smoke of the blood of the wise,
The holy, heroic, and good
Ascends from the earth to the skies,
And still crave the blood-hounds for blood.
How long shall injustice prevail?
And insult, and murder, and wrong,
Cause high-hearted Poland to wail?
Thou God of the helpless! how long?

1866.

A GOLDEN LOT.

In the coal-pit, or the factory,
　I toil by night or day,
And still to the music of labour
　I lilt my heart-felt lay;

I lilt my heart-felt lay—
　And the gloom of the deep, deep mine,
Or the din of the factory dieth away,
　And a Golden Lot is mine.

TO A STARTLED BIRD.

Fly not away, wee birdie, pray!
　No weasels we, no evil-bringers,
Would make thee bear the pangs that tear
　Too oft the hearts of sweetest singers.

Long may thy nest with eggs be blest,
　And prove with these brown four, yet fountains
Of tender lays to charm the days
　Of future climbers of the mountains.

Psychic Poems.

I.

THE VITAL SPARK:

AN INNER VOICE.

BEWILDERED by Life's Gordian Knot, long o'er me
  Despair had flung her adamantine chain,
When thro' the abyss of my spirit "Glory!"
  A deep voice cried, and "Glory!" then this strain :—

"A spark eternal from the co-eternal,
  And inner source of light ere time began,
The soul built from the dust its home external,
  And so became what we now know as man.

"The outer temple built, an inner, finer,
  From this and like to this was next ordained,
In which might be attained a life diviner
  Than could within the outer be attained.

"Thus in the image in man's form reflected,
  From out the universal Soul, the soul
Its individuality projected,
  And so became a whole within the whole.

" From root and knot, from knot and leaf to blossom,
  Upsprang by slow degrees the oak to view;
So by degrees as slow from out God's bosom,
  The vital spark to man immortal grew.

" The swaddles, that enswathe the babe, those swaddles
  Are rent asunder as we stronger grow;
And for the prate that pleased us in our cradles
  We're taught a higher, deeper lore to know.

" So by degrees man thus obtains his being,
  So by degrees his mental prime's obtained,
When grown from Man the Blind to Man the Seeing,
  The chains are rent in twain by which he's chained.

" Then from the chaos of the days primeval,
  Into the future far his ken extends—
Then to his ken what error seemed and evil
  Appear but instruments to noble ends.

"The shadow's self, thus seen, becomes a splendour,
  The mystic maze pervaded by a plan;
And laws sublime are seen to rule and render
  Harmonic what but discord seemed to man.

"In matter's seen the means to vanquish matter,
  In many a dismal ban a blessing bright;
In states chaotic, what their gloom might scatter,
  And their domains enshrine in living light.

"The darkest woe the brightest joy enclaspeth,
  In what seems false is seen the true, a power
Which grasped by man as rich a mace he graspeth,
  As ever graced the mythic gods of yore.

"A thinker clear nor less a doer; even
  A more than soul Titanic he, who still
Can make the very death-forged bolts of heaven
  To dance attendance on his potent will.

"The very lightning that the vision dazzles,
  The very tempest that the forest rends,
Are vassals bound unto his will, and vassals
  That help to realize the highest ends.

"Even as he wills empires arise—inventions
  Are seen uniting foreign land to land;
And where but winds and waves held dire contentions
  By sweetest intercourse the deeps are spann'd.

"A victor o'er the elements, a victor
  E'en over self he moves, till lo! appears
Upon the earth he treads the very picture
  Of what can be in the seraphic spheres.

"From higher than the seraph state descended,
    Up to the goal from whence he came he climbs;
And when the days of mortal life are ended,
    Still upward scales he thro' long future times.

"Just as the bee with honey laden flieth,
    To hive the guerdon earned by toil and pang;
So by experience enriched, he hieth
    With power to gift the Power from whom he sprang.

" Yea, ever moves he glory-ward, and ever
    Does glory to the Love Eterne accord!"
Thus rang that voice within my soul, and never
    Shall I forget how sweet the voice thus heard.

II.

THE DOWNFALL OF MAMMON;

OR, THE POET'S DREAM.

The baleful era of King Gold has vanished,
    And men disgusted with the part they played,
From out the temple of their hearts are banished
    The idols that debased the souls they swayed.

Man yet hath passions and the cause of passions,
    And so will have in his best future-state ;
But he hath reason too, by which he fashions
    Them into servants for a purpose great.

Instead of self-hood and of actions cruel,
    Inspired by Love heroic deeds abound ;
And Charity's esteemed a richer jewel
    Than ever yet in Orient mine was found.

Instead of falsehood, Truth his speech inspireth,
    Inspires his thought and permeates the man,
Till lo ! the utter'd word a worth acquireth
    Which merely written missives never can.

Instead of Superstition grim and hideous,
    Religion triumphs, and whate'er obtain,
No longer Envy can, with hints invidious,
    Cause man to visit brother man with pain.

Thus in ways manifold, sublime, and glorious,
    The God-sprung tenants of the earth at last,
Arise o'er every mortal ill victorious,
    That made their life a hell-life in the past.

No longer prompted by fell aspirations,
    Doth man send havoc into realms afar ;
But gains from acts of peace more prized ovations
    Than ever gratified the sons of war.

No longer to his inner part disloyal,
  He learneth, from the still small voice he scorn'd,
How to become a king in act, more royal
  Than ever yet a throne of gold adorn'd.

No longer bound to themes abhorr'd or hated,
  On highest subjects is the mind employed;
And as by war no Land is desolated,
  From lack of love no heart is left a void.

By cords of sympathy before the altar,
  Not chains of gold are youth and virgin led;
And when the trite "I will" their accents falter,
  From hearts 'tis falter'd in affection wed.

No want of union and no fatal duel
  Fought by two hearts in silence grim, if not
In cruel actions or in words as cruel,
  The lot of wedlock makes a bitter lot.

A circle round the hearth-stone, young and olden,
  The family gather, and their feelings blend
And interblend, till in a concord golden
  As one they labour for a noble end.

In time those circles form but inner circles
  To circles greater, till the Nations act
As one vast soul whose sphere with glory sparkles,
  And heaven, the dream on earth, is heaven the fact.

Onward and upward move the Nations, onward
  And ever upward thus the earth-born move,
Till, like the gilded fane that pointeth sunward,
  Their soul-flames touch the flames of those above.

Then, in a way hard to be comprehended,
  As hills are cleft were hills ere time began,
So are the barriers asunder rended
  Which kept apart the Angel and the Man.

Illumined by a light celestial, even
  To them the light beyond the Veil's unfurl'd;
And messages of import sweet are given
  Unto the outer from the inner world.

Not dead are found those whom by death seemed captured,
  Not tho' their dust be scattered by the wind—
Not dead but living, and with hearts enraptured,
  Still toiling for the dear ones left behind.

United, soul to loving soul united—
  Blent heaven and earth in one harmonic whole;
Glory to God shout one and all united,
  And halleluiah rings from pole to pole

The baleful era of King Gold is vanished;
  The idols that debased the soul they chain'd,
From out the temple of the heart are banished;
  And the Millenium's at last obtained.

III.

THE RIDDLE READ.

I THANK my God I ever lived to see the blessed day,
   When the spirit's immortality to me is rendered clear;
Not by a logic might be made some other tune to play,
   But by a flash of inner light too keen for doubt to bear.

Long, long can death, be death indeed? I asked 'mid doubts and fears;
   Long vainly groped in darkness for the jewels I had lost;
Long listened for an answer to the quest expressed in tears,
   And only found what to the heart a bitterer struggle cost.

Oft in the visions of the night, I saw their golden locks;
   I kiss'd their eyes as violets sweet when March with boisterous breath,
The lordly oak itself—nay more, the lordly steeple rocks,
   And ever as the morn arose I found them fast in death.

Then said I—if the "be all" and the "end all" of this strife,
   Be but to furnish coronals the temples to adorn
Of Life's imperious Enemy, then, death, and not for life,
   Should be the boon solicited whene'er a babe is born.

Far better man had never been, if in a circle he
  Must travel till the little hour of mortal life is run,
To find when Life's dark riddle's read he then must cease
    to be,
  And the end of all his trouble is the end where he begun.

To labour in a night on which the sun will never rise—
  To sweat and groan without a hope shall end the bitter
    curse,
Save in a dissolution which shall only close our eyes
  On all we love and cherish—all?—what destiny were
    worse?

Nor worse were e'en the lot of those the Danaides of yore,
  Condemn'd the hole-fill'd tanks to fill from which the
    waters gushed
As fast as they the fluid in poured or could the fluid in
    pour,
  And left them only for their pains a heart by anguish
    crush'd.

Not worse to be like Ixion doom'd on a wheel to spin,
  Transfix'd on which the victim sad arrived at every round,
Just where he did the weary, dizzy, dreary round begin,
  Which he—the sore confounded—served the deeper to
    confound.

Not worse to be like Sisyphus, destined up a high hill,
  With many an effort, many a pang, still to uproll a rock,
Which when the goal was all but won, despite an iron will,
  Re-bounded in a way that made his labours vast, a mock.

Not worse to be like these, for these, amid their night of pain,
    Had intervals of hope that would the darkest hour illume;
But what avails to charm the soul who loves and toils—and then
    Learns not a vestige of his ME can pass beyond the tomb?

In vain to point the present—what can the present yield,
    Except what proves a mock, and still the heart with sorrow fills?   [shield
And without the charm a Future Life affords, without a
    The soul is left to battle with the worst of human ills.

In vain to point the past, in vain, will not its sheen arise
    Upon the mind about to be in death's dark cradle rock'd,
To keener make the thought that when the vital sparklet flies,   [lock'd?
Lock'd lies the spirit in the bonds in which the sense is

To die and be no more is more than we can think, without
    An effort such as rends the heart or petrifies the man;
And when the soul has once began to tread the plain of Doubt,
    The valley of Despair is reached before we halt, or can.

Thus felt I till the truth was found by patient labour sought,
    —By labour and a spirit framed to brook the world's harsh scorn;   [fraught,
When gilded by its sheen a soul was mine with rapture
    And may be yours who seek aright the truths I sought to learn.

IV.

THE MISSION.

"I HAVE oped my inner vision,"
(Spake the Spirit to the Seer,)
"Now I'll show to thee the mission
Which whate'er betides—whate'er—
Thou by heaven's high permission shalt accomplish.—Give
    ear!

"Thou shalt write and speak, and wholly
By the gift of speech and song,
Thou shalt make the proud one lowly,
And the weak in spirit, strong,
And the servitor of folly for the ways of wisdom long.

"Thou shalt teach, he who devises
Harm for others, harm will meet;
And that he who most despises
Counsel's—to himself a cheat;
That the wisest of the wise is most devoid of self-conceit.

"Thou shalt speak a word in season
To the poor in bondage, nor
Forget to say 'tis treason
'Gainst the highest to ignore
The claims of love and reason, and to trample on the poor.

"Thou shalt teach the tyrant master
  How to view his servant's lot;
Not to want the wheels go faster
  Then there's strength to do it—not—
Not to make it a disaster to be cradled in a cot.

"Thou shalt teach the willing toiler,
  Doomed for fee to shape and plan,
He has that which no despoiler
  May divest him of—nor can—
The power to make his scorner feel the dignity of man.

"Thou shalt tell the sordid miser
  Not heaps of guinea gold
Will ever make him wiser—
  For wisdom ne'er was sold,
And lacking which his joys are too meagre to be told.

"Ask what will be his measure,
  When dust to dust's restored;
What shall serve his gold, what pleasure
  Shall gems the soul afford?
And if his worshipped treasure shall be worth one tender word.

"The brighest jewels sparkling
  In the courts above,
Are the deeds encircling
  The heart enshrined in love,
And lacking which we darkling down, ever downward, move.

"All this in words unvarnished,
　　Say to the world ; and say,
That lives by deeds ungarnished
　　Must be deplored—and may
As much as lives crime-tarnished, which other traits display.

"Strike, strike at superstition !
　　Bid its slaves with open eyes,
See, in lack of a volition
　　For themselves to think, there lies
A more damnable perdition than the bigots can devise.

" Bid each for himself but ponder,
　　And e'en though he err, persist ;
And the fetters he will sunder,
　　That now threaten to resist ;
Nay, e'er long he'll come to wonder how so long he lay in mist.

" Risen on the wings of rapture,
　　At his freedom, he will soar
Far 'yond the reach of Scripture
　　Misconstruers, evermore
To redazzle, to recapture by their guile-engendered lore.

"Leaving churches and their minions,
　　Leaving books and bells and beads,
Leaving Craftdom's dark dominions
　　To the bigots and their creeds,
He will stamp his bold opinions on the coin of golden deeds.

"Thus thy thought shall like a sabre
    Cut some knot, if not untie,
  And some duty to a neighbour
    Do—and yet a nobler—ay,
A higher, holier labour must thy efforts yet employ.

"See, yon desolated woman
    Weeping o'er an infant lost;
  Tearing out her hair, consuming
    Life in anguish, till a ghost
She seems and not a woman weeping o'er her baby lost.

"Go, take her hand extended—
    In words of music say,
  How the spirit that descended
    Once on Pentecost, yet may
The bosom heal thus rended—say the child's not far away.

"Say, In fact the little jewel
    Not a clod sepulchred lies—
  Ah, the cruel creed, the cruel
    Hearts can teach such creed unwise!
That her jewel, yet a jewel will sparkle in her eyes.

"Aloud let it be sounded,
    Whoever were, yet are;
  Not lost in space unbounded,
    Not in another star—
That yet around, about us are the friends we deem afar.

"This may sound like a gigantic
  Fiction to the world—'tis true;
And thou be held an antic,
  And bigots not a few
Will with a fury frantic thy lonely steps pursue.

"Slander black, and black detraction,—
  All the poison'd darts of hate,
All the malice of a faction
  Whose wounded pride would sate
Itself on thy distraction, to brook shall be thy fate.

"But thou shalt stand undaunted,
  The arrows at thee hurl'd,
Till on Falsehood's grave implanted
  The flag of Truth's unfurl'd,
And a mighty pæan's chanted by her angels to the world.

"That shall be a day of glory—
  Glory to our God on high—
  Glory to the angels o'er ye—
  Glory and exceeding joy—
Glory to the Nations—glory to the seer they'd now destroy.

"Thus I've oped thy inner vision—
  In the language of thy kind
Have shown to thee the mission
  For which thou art designed—
Then go, and with God's blessing do the work to thee assigned."

V.

BEHIND THE VEIL.

A PHANTOM to me thou appearest;
But, spite of this seeming, I know,
The magical image thou wearest
Is real as the lilies in blow —
Is as real and as fair as the fairest of all our fair lilies in blow.

Not alive to the senses external
Of hearing, the touch, or the sight;
Not aught that would yield to the carnal
Desire, a delusive delight;
But alive to the spirit art thou and a star to its path day night.

Not alive to the outer, but inner
Keen sense of the spirit; and when
I'm from the world and its din or
Low chat of most women and men,
I'm mantled thro' thee in a glory, no pencil could portray, nor pen.

Then lifted on Rapture's bright pinions
I tread the bright zones of the Blest;
I enter the azure dominions
Of those who have long been at rest
From turmoil, the strife, the opinions, by which here the Good are opprest.

Away o'er the gold-crested mountains,
   I hie, light of foot as the roe ;
   I drink of the pellucid fountains
     That flow in the valleys below,
And swiftly both valleys and mountains with the deepest significance glow.

   Then see I expressed in those valleys;
   Then see I enthroned in those hills;
   In dew-adorned daffodowndillies,
     And daisies that bloom by the rills—
I see one vast Soul, and that all is but what that inherent Soul wills.

   Then see I—But what serves the vision
     Of music-souled bard, seer, or sage,
   When Bigotry, Self, Superstition,
     Unite their fell forces to wage
A war upon Truth? Truth divine! and when Learning would fetter the age!

   What, what would it be to the nations
     Did I give what I'd give for Love's sake?
   Would they hark to the blest revelations
     I'd deem it my duty to make?
They'd say I had drank of a potion should doom me to dungeon or stake.

Yet freely this much may be spoken,
    That when from her dungeon of clay
—A bird from its fetterlet broken—
    The soul to the spheres wings away,
We find where go not a token of what our learned bigots portray.

There find we in joy or in sorrow
    No day without night, as we're told;
No, no night on which dawneth no morrow;
    But the scrolls of the past are unroll'd,
And we see, as if shown in a mirror, each fact there is there to unfold.

On all can be seen by the spirit
    Around us, above, or below;
Nay even the homes we inherit,
    Are graced or defaced, gloom or glow
With merit, our merit, demerit; our joy or shame, glory or woe.

Not in dead pictures merely, but living
    Bright symbols our deed speak and move;
And we see with the gifts we have given,
    In the God-enshrined spirit of love,
The least of our sins, tho' forgiven, can never be cancelled Above.

There see we the unborn Hereafter,
   From out the live Present is born ;
That laughers are reft of their laughter,
   The mask from the masker is torn ;
The crafty are whipt by their craft and the scorner is met by his scorn.

We learn this, but learn too, whatever
   The strength and the hue of our creed,
A good deed's a good deed, and never
   Can other be than a good deed ;
That Destiny's self cannot sever nor keep from the worthy their meed.

To clear-sighted psychist is granted
   All this and things deeper to know,
That in accents of fire should be chanted
   To creed-ridden mortals below,
Could feelings by which I am haunted, be taught in bright numbers to flow.

But of this I despair ; and I wander
   With one, once a mortal, to find
The marvels we see, and their grandeur
   Can never be shown to mankind,
Till each for himself's learned to ponder, and feel the sad fact, he is blind.

VI.

WHAT IS MAN?

WHAT is man? The question floweth
    From the lips with ease, and yet
He who best could answer knoweth
    Answer true were hard to get:
Not the Sphinx in Egypt olden,
    Did a deeper question ask:
Love to strengthen and embolden
    Be to answer mine the task.

But a feeble mortal merely;
    An immortal now believed:
One too complex to be clearly
    Even by himself conceived:
One both complex and immortal
    Say I inward going—yea;—
Death is but to Life the portal,
    As the poets always say.

From the inner sun a sparklet
    He (Man) glows a star in turn,
From whose life evolving circlet
    Other living powers are born;
This a meteor, that a starlet,
    Burn they while years take wing;
To the cheek the guilt-born scarlet,
    Or the glow of bliss to bring.

Yea, let Empires pass; the granite
    Boulder moulder into clay;
From their pathway star and planet
    And their splendour pass away,
Yet when these have sped, each action,
    And each thought we prize or rue,
To our rapture or distraction
    Shall the soul immortal view.

Not our merit or dismerit,
    But to crown or punish—ne'er;
In the regions of the spirit,
    Other ends life's issues bear.
Deeper than the ocean, even,
    Higher than Orion still—
Still to them the power is given,
    On to go for good or ill.

Boundless yet for good and evil;
    Not for good or evil—loth,
Loth were truth to call him devil,
    Man's a god and devil both.
But the devil weakens, stronger
    In his soul the god-head grows,
Till a slave to sin no longer,
    On Life's chequered way he goes.

Up thro' ill the good still rises,
    And the souls thus risen see
What oft hid from dimmer eyes, is
    Without ill no good can be.

Nay, thro' strife with the infernal,
 And the sinful only can,
In the courts of the Eternal,
 Be a high seat won by Man.

From the shattered limbs of Cælus
 Given to the ocean waves,
Venus rose, as legends tell us,
 She whose grace the heart enslaves.
So thro' life with evil shatter'd,
 May we seem a moment, when,
Lo! from out the relics scattered
 Springs what's hailed a God to Men.

What is Man? You have my answer,
 In a may be less prized song,
Than a tip-toed, tight-rope dance, were
 By yon wonder stricken throng.
Yet however weak it seemeth
 'Tis from one the truth would know,
And for Truth's advantage streameth—
 Would all lauded songs did so.

VII.

THE SOUL'S HEREAFTER.

Dies not the soul when dust to dust is given ;
Even as we are in earth-life are we still,
Save from the worn-out garment rent and riven,
That may have proved a fetter to the will.

Not unto demons void of good converted,
Not unto angels void of error—no ;
But human-spirited, and human-hearted,
We on our way with pain or pleasure go.

Not reft of feeling—nay, with feelings keener
To others' woes, more keen to others' joys ;
With bosoms purer and with minds serener—
Though human still, more humane we and wise.

Not more to be despised, nor venerated,
For aught from change of state acquired or caught
But at our inner value estimated,
Shall we be shunned or courted as we ought.

Not to their fabled hell, nor fabled heaven,
By the good Father's will are we consigned,
But to a sphere of human action—even,
To one adapted to each frame and mind.

Not one sweet feeling passeth unrewarded
Not one black deed can go unpunished—not—
Not one swift thought can vanish unrecorded
And give no colour to our future lot.

Not words but thoughts, and not on faith but actions,
And on whatever gives our acts their hue,
The heart's allurements, and the mind's distractions—
Is based the verdict we shall prize or rue.

Yes, such the future that awaits the spirit;
Then let us pause and think while pause we can,
How best we may the meed eternal merit,
That shall be to the weal eterne of man.

VIII.

THE INNER CONFLICT.

Thrice "Iö Pæan!" let me cry,
    And bless the hour that I was born;
And born thro' love in vain to sigh—
    To cheer my longing heart a morn
Has risen in my ebon sky,
    Such as did ne'er my sky adorn;
And now with shout triumphant, lo!
A victor on my way I go.

A tenant of some curse-girt sphere
  Long seem'd I—even so—and Pain
Still by a destiny severe,
  Had power my spirit to enchain,
Or to impel his venomed spear
  Up to the hilt in heart and brain ;
And this he did—but this once done,
The measure of his power was run—

Yea, having brooked the worst, I felt
  The power within, with steadfast gaze,
To scan the blows upon me dealt,—
  Life's issues to their cause to trace ;
And whilst I looked, the fogs did melt
  That swathed my ken—and face to face
I stood with Fate's own self and viewed
The secret of the lash I'd rued.

Illumined by an inner light,
  My past a pictured scroll became,
In which my sorrow, my delight,
  My hope, my fear, my pride, my shame,
Assumed a shape and colour quite
  Beyond the power of speech to name—
A chronicle mysterious, man
Engrossed by self might never scan.

Yet gazing on that mystic scroll,
　Enough of its contents was read,
To teach my desolated soul,
　Not all in vain she'd pined and bled
Beneath the lash, the dire control
　Of passions fierce, by beauty fed;—
Nor yet in vain her longings—if
She read aright this hieroglyph.

This learned I from that scroll, and learned
　The way by which to rend the chain
Had kept my soul in self inurned:
　Unhappy self that would obtain,
Whatever won is ever mourn'd,
　Whose blessings e'er as bans remain—
Ah, would that men would reck this reed,
So would their hearts less often bleed.

With feelings sharpened—eye and ear—
　For others weal I then did learn
To shed the sympathetic tear,
　To wile the frown from temples stern;
To do the thing desired to cheer,
　To speak the word required to warn;
And in return a boon did find,
In all appeals to heart and mind.

Ay, with the All-enwoven—both
　The outer and the inner world
Did I survey—e'en in the froth
　By Life's imperious surges hurled
In its unutterable wroth,
　As worthy only to be furl'd
In limbo's bosom—on Time's sands,
A sheen that seen the soul expands.

That glory in the grass, as sung
　By deep-souled bard, and in the flower
A glamour o'er my spirit flung,
　And strove—nor vainly—to re-dower
Her with that bliss from which we sprung,
　When in creation's natal hour
God said, "Let there be Light!"—and up
She leapt enraptured with Life's cup.

Then "Iö Pæan!" let me cry,
　And bless the hour that I was born,
And born thro' Love to languish—ay,
　To curse that natal hour—a morn
Has risen in my spirit's sky,
　Such as did ne'er that sky adorn;
And now with shout triumphant, lo!
A victor on my way I go.

IX.

THE THOUGHT TOILER.

A THOUGHT TOILER, faint and o'ercome by his labours,
And the manifold troubles by which he was girt,
Combined with the titters and sneers of his neighbours,
Lost heart, and thus vented the pangs of his heart :—

" I'm a-weary with care, I'm a-weary with care,
Surrounded with woes that no mortal can bear,
Whilst I gaze on the night of my ills and survey,
Not a star to direct my lorn soul on its way.

" I'm shorn of my strength, and the few are my years,
The winter of life on my aspect appears ;
Ay, the feeling of death steals apace round my core,
Like the sea-waves around yon lone rock on the shore."

So rang the wild wail, when a voice from the spheres,
Where dwell the good angels, awoke on his ears—
" Refrain from thy tears, from thy sorrows refrain,
The gloom that engirts thee shall vanish again.

"Tho' in shadows the car of thy destiny's driven,
And thy hopes are extinguished, thy bosom-chords riven,
Not, not in one battle for right hast thou striven
Unwitness'd by God and the angels of heaven.

"And could but thy eyes now be open'd as they
Will be open'd, and not in a far distant day,
Thou would'st see for thy trials, a guerdon more bright
Than the jewels that garnish the mantle of night.

"For the lava of thought that has sparkled and burned,
In thy innermost soul's to a diadem turned;
And every tear thou hast shed is a gem,
That enhances the worth of that rare diadem.

"And every sigh thou hast breathed to a tone
Far sweeter than music on waters has grown;
And that music will flow in thy new-opened ears,
With a might that shall lead thee to bless the past years.

"Ah, then shalt thou see not in vain hast thou wept;
Not in vain hast thou laboured whilst others have slept;
Not in vain hast thou sorrowed whilst others entranced
With the pleasures that perish have giggled and danced.

"And every trouble and every burden,
And every pang thou hast felt and endured,
Shalt thou find," cried the voice, "has its own precious guerdon!"
And the Toiler at this to his strength was restored.

X.

THE GUARDIAN ANGEL.

I'M the spirit Emmalina, thy guardian angel, and
Drawn hither by a subtle law but few can understand—
The golden cord of sympathy, I leave the summer-land,
  Thy aching brows with lilies to entwine.

I've watched thee late and early, I've watched thee on the morn;
And when the sun has left the sky, and Luna like a lorn
Dejected maid has brought the hour most prized by hearts, grief-torn,
  I thy aching brows with lilies have entwined.

I've watched thee in the battle with the many ills of Life,
And then when sleep has seized thee, only to renew the strife   [and rife,
In dreams, has made, thy woe too rife, appear more keen
  I thy aching brows with lilies have entwined.

I've watched when dark and dreary has been thy horoscope;
And when thou strength has needed most with cark and care to cope,   [of hope—
I've nerved thy arm, into thy heart have poured the oil
  I thy aching brows with lilies have entwined.

1878.

END OF PSYCHIC POEMS.

NOTE.

I HAVE been solicited to say a few words about the author of this book, and I think that his readers will be sufficiently interested to wish to know something about him. As we have been intimate friends for more than twenty years, I have not much difficulty in the task.

The poems must stand or fall upon their merits. The conditions under which they have been produced do not affect their literary value. But so far as form and style go, the critic will only be able to come to a sound judgment when he knows something of those conditions. The author is a Northumbrian born and bred; his speech is racy of the soil. Northumbrian pronunciation is other and older than that which obtains amongst our south-country kinsfolk; this must be borne in mind when in these poems a rhyme may seem uncouth or even non-existent; it is probably only to our manner born. A south-country Englishman may read even Robert Burns's finest verses as though they had but little of the jingle of rhyme about them.

Joseph Skipsey has passed the greater part of his life in coal mines; he comes of a mining race. Having lost his father when yet a child in arms, and his widowed mother having seven other children to care for, he had to begin work early. At seven years of age he was sent into the coal pits at Percy Main, near North Shields. Young as he was, he had to work from twelve to sixteen hours in the day, generally in the pitch-dark; and in the dreary winter months he only saw the blessed sun upon Sundays. But he had a brave heart; he was paving his way, and he was determined to get wisdom. When he went to work, he had learned the alphabet, and to put words of two letters together, but nothing more. He devoted such scanty opportunities of leisure as he could get to learning to read, write, and cypher. He was his own schoolmaster. He taught himself to write, for example, by copying the letters from printed bills or notices, when he could manage to get a candle end,—his paper being the trap-door, which it was his duty to open and shut as the waggons passed through, and his pen a bit of chalk.

The first book he really read was the "Bible," and not content with reading it, he learned the chapters which specially pleased him by heart. When sixteen years old he was presented with an old copy of Lindley Murray's Grammar, and by the aid of that unrivalled, if old-fashioned work, he gained some knowledge of the structural rules of his native tongue. He had already become acquainted with "Paradise Lost," and was another proof of the truth of Matthew Prior's axiom, "Who often reads will sometimes want to write," for he had begun to write verse when only "a bonnie pit lad."

I need not follow his subsequent career in detail. For more than forty years of his life he has laboured in "the coal-dark underground;" he has had a short experience of storekeeping in a manufactory, and of acting as assistant in a public library; and is now the caretaker of a Board School in Newcastle-upon-Tyne,—an office of much labour and small emolument, which affords its fortunate possessor little opportunity of lettered ease.

I must say a word or two more about Joseph Skipsey himself,— for we have in him a man of mark, a man who has made himself, and has done it well. His life-long devotion to literary pursuits has never been allowed to interfere with the proper discharge of his daily duties. Whilst still a working pitman he was master of his craft, and it took an exceptionally good man to match him as a hewer of coal. When, after many long years of patient toil, he won his way to an official position, he gained the respect of those above him in authority whilst retaining the confidence and affection of the men. Simple, straight, and upright, he has held his own wherever he has been placed. Since he left the mine he has, among other things, edited as well as written several of the introductory biographies and critical notices of the *Canterbury Poets* Series for Mr. Walter Scott.

For such work he has peculiar qualifications. He has read much and has thought carefully; he has gone to the works themselves, and has formed his conclusions upon them for himself; and his critical judgments have a freshness and a value which are all their own. Few men have a more thorough knowledge of our literature from the Elizabethan period downwards; and by patient and diligent study of their best work, in various translations, he has gained an intimate acquaintance with several of the greatest writers of the Continent. It is an intellectual treat to hear our pitman-poet discuss such questions as the comparative merits of the "Jew of Malta" and "Shylock," the necessity of the second part of "Faust," or the comparative value amongst poets of Wordsworth and Shelley, with men of high and acknowledged literary position and attainments, and more than hold his own.

It is not for me to enter upon a criticism of my friend's poems, but I may perhaps be allowed to say that one great merit of many of them lies in the fact that in them he is dealing with the most vivid aspects of that strange, uncertain, hazardous, and interesting calling with which he is practically familiar. He speaks in them as only one who knows can speak,—straight from the heart to the heart. Take the two verses named, "Get Up." How simple, strong, and true they are—not a word which could be spared nor a word too few; and yet as suggestive, as picturesque, as full of food for much thought, as any two verses you will find, no matter who the singer. The life of the miner is one of peril; he lives with his own and the lives of those dear to him constantly in his hand; and Joseph Skipsey has had bitter and painful experience of the cruel sorrows to which he is exposed.

NOTE.

He is personally known to not a few of the men whom, in letters and art, England delights to honour, and I think I may truly say that he is "honoured of them all." Perhaps, if we could see things as they really are, Joseph Skipsey is the best product of the north-country coal-fields since George Stephenson held his safety-lamp in the blower at Killingworth pit.

R. SPENCE WATSON.

January 1886.

Printed by WALTER SCOTT, *Felling, Newcastle-on-Tyne.*

NOTE.

THE RING, page 49.—There is a tradition that Essex had elicited from Queen Elizabeth a ring as a token of confidence, with the assurance that if ever he should incur her displeasure, or need her assistance, by the production of the said ring she should be pacified, or that assistance given. Afterwards the Earl was impeached for high treason, tried, and condemned, when to the last the Queen anxiously awaited the forthcoming of the token which should have secured his pardon. The talisman did not come, and the Earl was executed. Years after, the Queen discovered that the Earl had, by a confidant, sent to her the ring, but that from malicious motives it had not been delivered, whereat she went nearly frantic, and died a few days after of a broken heart.

THE END.

www.ingramcontent.com/pod-product-compliance
Lightning Source LLC
Chambersburg PA
CBHW031943230426
43672CB00010B/2026